Into the Pacific Wo

MICHAEL HAIGH

CAMBRIDGE UNIVERSITY PRESS
Cambridge
New York Port Chester Melbourne Sydney

Published by the Press Syndicate of the University of Cambridge
The Pitt Building, Trumpington Street, Cambridge CB2 1RP
40 West 20th Street, New York, NY 10011, USA
10 Stamford Road, Oakleigh, Melbourne 3166, Australia

First published 1984
Reprinted 1987
Second edition 1989

Printed in Hong Kong by Wing King Tong

Library of Congress catalogue card number: 89–564

British Library cataloguing in publication data
Haigh, Michael
Into the Pacific world. – 2nd ed. (New
routes in GCSE geography).
1. Pacific region. Human geographical
features
I. Title II. Series
304.2′09182′3

ISBN 0 521 35783 7
(First edition ISBN 0 521 28604 2)

Cover photograph: Milford Sound, South Island, New Zealand

Acknowledgements

The author and publisher would like to thank the following for permission to use their photographs:

Japan Weather Association 1; The Australian Information Service 4–7, 9–11, 14, 15, 17 bottom, 18 (London), 21 (Melbourne); Qantas Airways Ltd 8; Government of Queensland 12; Government of Western Australia 13, 16, 22; Government of New South Wales 17 top, 19 left; L. Swain 19 right; Overseas Containers Ltd 23; New Zealand High Commission front cover and 24, 25 top, 29, 30, 32, 34–36, 37 top, 39–41; The Alexander Turnbull Library 25 bottom, 26, 27; M.P. King 28, 37 bottom; CNZ Photo Agency, Wellington, NZ 31, 33 top; National Publicity Studios, Wellington, NZ 33 bottom; New Zealand Aluminium Smelters 38; Ishikawajima–Harima Heavy Industries Co Ltd 42 top, 52 top, 53; Japan Graphic Inc 42 bottom (Laboratory of Urban Safety Planning), 44 top (Chunichi Newspapers), 64; Associated Press 44 bottom; Japan Information Centre (London) 46, 47, 58 top, 63 top left, top right, bottom; Nippon Steel Corpn 51; Hitachi Zosen 52 bottom; Nissan Motor Co Ltd 54; Toyota Motor Corpn 55; IBM 56; Sony (UK) Ltd 57; Sasebo Heavy Industries Co Ltd 58 bottom; Mitsubishi Heavy Industries Ltd 60; Japan National Tourist Organization 61, 65; Japanese National Railways 62, 63 top right, centre; Japan Information Centre (London) 58 top, 63 top left, top centre, bottom; Anglo-Chinese Educational Institute 66, 67, 68 bottom, 69 left, 71–73, 74 bottom, 75 right, 76 top, 77 bottom, 78, 83; Monique Vanstone 68 top, 69 right, 70 right, 76 bottom, 79 top, 80–82; Hutchison Library 70 left, 77 top; Robert Withnall 74 top, 75 left, bottom; China Shenzken Photography Institute News Photo Agency 79 bottom; Hong Kong Tourist Association 84, 88 top, 89 bottom; Hong Kong Government Office 85 bottom, 86, 87, 88 bottom, 89 top; Singapore Tourist Promotion Board 90, 92; Jurong Town Corporation 93, 94, 95.

Contents

Australia

1 *Sydney Cove, 1788*

Developing a remote continent

Europeans were not sure that Australia was there until Dutch sailors landed on its west and south coasts in the seventeenth century. They were merchants who would sail great distances in dangerous seas to make their fortunes from gold and spices which they could sell in Europe. They found a barren land which they decided to avoid in future.

2 *Spread of the graziers*

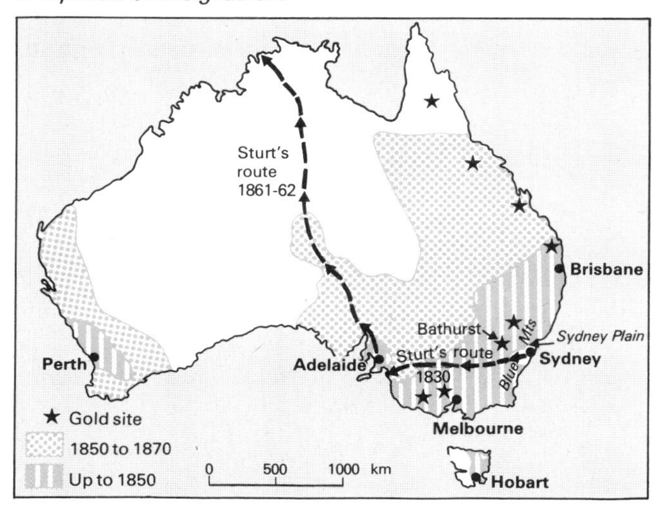

In 1768, when Britain was becoming more powerful, Captain James Cook went in search of this southern continent. On 29th April 1770, he landed on the east coast of Australia and claimed for Britain the land he called New South Wales.

In May 1787, eleven ships set sail from Britain, carrying 760 convicts and 270 soldiers and sailors. Eight months later, the ships arrived in Australia. Illustration (1) shows the settlement at Sydney Cove in August 1788. Britain was sending people to the other side of the world to empty her crowded prisons and to develop a new land. The government hoped that these men and women would produce sailcloth and timber for the ships of the British Navy. This idea was soon dropped because the land was found to be very poor.

Each year more convicts were sent to Australia, and within twenty-five years there were over 30 000 people living on the Sydney Plain. In 1813, the first explorers crossed the Blue Mountains and found low hills and wide plains covered with open woodland and grass – ideal lands for raising sheep. The explorer Charles Sturt led the way from the Sydney settlement into the continent. Graziers with their sheep followed his trail. Map (2) shows Sturt's route and the spread of the graziers.

The number of sheep grew from 1 million in 1830 to 20 million in 1850. The wool was sent to Yorkshire in Britain which led the world in making wool cloth. Australia had become a useful colony providing the wool for Britain's industry.

Free settlers from Britain began to arrive in large numbers and coastal settlements grew rapidly. These are shown on map (2) and in table (3).

3 Foundation dates of settlements

Settlement	*Year founded*
Hobart	1803
Brisbane	1824
Perth	1829
Melbourne	1835
Adelaide	1836

4 Where Aboriginals lived

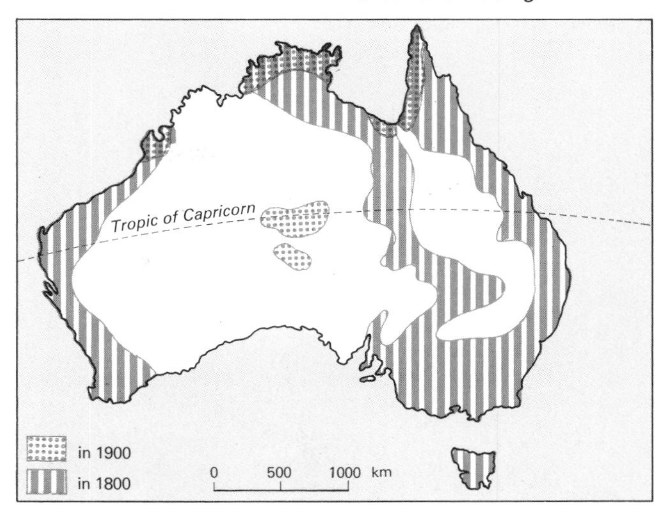

Graziers and Aboriginals

When the first convicts arrived in Australia there were 300 000 Aboriginals living in about 600 tribal groups. Map (4) shows where they lived in 1800 and in 1900.

Most Aboriginals lived in the south-east where the new settlers were spreading. They were soon to suffer at the hands of the newcomers, who were discovering the land the Aboriginals had known for 40 000 years.

Whole tribes were massacred by the graziers. Many died from diseases such as influenza, smallpox and measles brought by the Europeans. Others exchanged their land for a few blankets, trinkets and knives. Photograph (5) shows the explorer John Batman securing the future site of Melbourne from the local Aboriginal tribe in 1835.

In 1851, gold was found in Bathurst, and within ten years three-quarters of a million people flocked to Australia to make their fortunes.

When all the surface deposits had been worked in the south, the gold diggers set off to find gold in the north. They went into hot wet lands which sheep rearers avoided. Here, sheep suffered from pests and diseases, lambing was difficult and the wool was poor quality. Beef cattle fared better on the tropical grasses, and stockmen with their herds followed the gold diggers. On their way they took more land from the Aboriginals.

The centre of Australia was still unknown to the settlers. Explorers hoped that they would find an inland sea surrounded by fresh pastures. John Stuart trekked across the continent along the route shown on map (2). He found some pasture lands but no inland sea. Those who went west found only desert. In 1879, graziers discovered water under the ground. Wells were dug to water the thirsty animals which could now be kept on every patch of grass which they could find. By 1890, 100 million sheep and 12 million cattle were grazing freely on Australia's pasture. But only 40 000 Aboriginals were left, most of them in the dry interior and tropical coastlands where the settlers did not want to live.

5 John Batman secures the future site of Melbourne, 1835

FOLLOW-UP WORK

1 Copy the map (2) showing the spread of the graziers. Colour the map like this.
   Original area of settlement around Sydney – *red*
   Extent of grazing up to 1850 – *dark green*
   Extension of grazing between 1850 and 1870 – *light green*
2 Join up the gold sites with an arrowed line, showing the Pacific Gold Trail from south to north.
3 Draw a line graph to show the growth of the Australian population using the statistics in table (6). Plot the population on the vertical axis, using a scale of 100 000 per centimetre.

6 Growth of population

Year	*Population*
1801	5 900
1811	11 900
1821	35 500
1831	76 000
1841	221 000
1851	437 700
1861	1 168 100
1871	1 700 900

4 Explain the sharp rise in population
   (a) in the 1830s,
   (b) in the 1850s.
5 Study the position of Australia on a world map. Explain why this section describes Australia as a remote continent.
6 Suggest reasons why the earliest settlements were located on the coast.
7 What stopped the graziers with their sheep from spreading
   (a) further north,
   (b) further west?
8 Study map (4).
   (a) Why do you think the area that the graziers settled was an area where many Aboriginals lived?
   (b) In which parts of the continent were the Aboriginals not disturbed by the new settlers?
9 'The spread of the graziers was a disaster for the Aborigine race.' Do you agree? Give reasons for your answer.

ABORIGINALS (ABORIGINES)

The original native people who were living in a region before the arrival of colonists.

7 Mining bauxite at Weipa

Modern developments and the Aboriginals

There were 160 000 Aboriginals in 1988. Over half live in towns and cities. About 50 000 Aboriginals lead a tribal life on reserves set aside for them. There are 350 reserves with a total area which is 8 per cent of Australia and twice the size of Britain. On these reserves, a few people live as nomads but most have settled and need government help to survive. Many Aboriginals work as stockmen on cattle stations.

In recent years minerals have been found on the reserves, and the Aboriginals face a new threat.

Each state has its own policy towards the Aboriginals. In Queensland, for example, Aboriginals were moved from their reserve to allow mining of bauxite to take place at Weipa (7). In South Australia, on the other hand, the Pitjantjatjara Aboriginals have a 20 per cent stake in the profits of oil developments on land which the State recognises belongs to them. The agreement also guarantees that Aboriginal sacred places and communities will not be disturbed by the developments.

FOLLOW-UP WORK

Study these statements.

(a) Minerals on Aboriginal reserves should be developed by mining companies for export and for Australia's industries.
(b) The Aboriginals should be trained to develop the minerals, so that they can develop their society.
(c) Mining companies should be allowed to develop minerals, but some of the profits should go to the Aboriginals.
(d) Minerals on reserves should not be developed.

Which statement do you agree with? Give reasons for your decision.

Land of migrants

About 160 000 convicts were taken to Australia between 1788 and 1853 when transportation came to an end. We have seen how the discovery of gold at that time brought a flood of new immigrants including thousands of Chinese coolies and diggers, which helped to raise Australia's population from 400 000 in 1850 to more than 2 million in 1880. When the goldfields declined, people turned to the land and became farmers. Until the end of the Second World War, almost all immigrants came from the British Isles. A cheap passage, cheap land, the promise of a better life, and the thrill of adventure, guaranteed a steady flow of free settlers. The journey to Australia in those days took months by sailing ship (8) and was very dangerous, as the details of one such journey show (9).

8 Sailing ships, Sydney 1870

FOLLOW-UP WORK

1 Plot the route of the *Duchess of Argyle* onto an outline map of the world.
2 What were the main problems of reaching Australia by sailing ship?

> *MIGRATION*
>
> The movement of people from one place to another. Movements may be internal – within a country – or external – from one country to another. Movement out of a country is called emigration and movement into a country is called immigration.

THE AUSTRALIA RUN SHIPPING GAME

You own a sailing ship which works out of the port of Liverpool. Rival companies want to capture your trade on the Australia run. Ask for details of the game.

9 Journey to Australia, 1886

SHIP: The Duchess of Argyle — TYPE: Sailing Ship — JOURNEY: Liverpool to Melbourne

CREW: 38 — PASSENGERS: 46 — English 40, Irish 6 — Single men 24, Married couples 3 — Single women 10, Children 6

DATE	POSITION	LATITUDE	LONGITUDE	CONDITIONS AND EVENTS
Nov. 16 1886	Liverpool	53 N	3 W	Fair weather. 16 stowaways put ashore
Nov. 26	Bay of Biscay	47 N	8 W	Rough seas. Ship rolling dangerously
Dec. 12	Equator	0	27 W	Hot. Calm seas. Heavy downpours of rain
Dec. 18	Close to Island of Trinidad	20 s	29 W	Very hot. Favourable winds. Problem of rats, lice and fleas
Dec. 28	Close to Island of Tristan da Cunha	35 s	12 W	Cold. Strong seas. Two sails blown away
Jan. 3 1887	Off the Cape of Good Hope	35 s	21 E	Mountainous seas. Topsail blown away
Jan. 12	South Indian Ocean	38 s	50 E	Dreadfully rough. Sail spars break. Ship trembles
Jan. 27	Approaching Australia	39 s	105 E	Some calm weather. Fog and cold. Sailmaker died
Feb. 7	300 miles from Melbourne	39 s	138 E	Headwinds since Jan 30. Slow progress
Feb. 12	Close to Cape Otway lighthouse	39 s	143 E	Ship driven close to shore. Nearly wrecked
Feb 15	Port Melbourne	38 s	145 E	See a barren land. Take train to Melbourne

Australia's population grew to 7 million at the start of the Second World War but when Japanese troops landed in New Guinea in 1942, Australians realised that their country was empty and vulnerable. Even with assisted passages costing no more than £10, sufficient numbers could not be raised from Britain alone to improve defence and settle more land. Australia opened her doors to Europeans such as Italians and Greeks who often lived in poverty in their own countries and who would be able to find work on new development projects such as the Snowy Mountains Scheme (see page 14). When one family arrived, a chain migration of friends and relatives quickly followed.

No state accepted people from nearby countries in Asia because they were considered a threat. Since Britain joined the EEC, and Australian trade with Japan and other Asian countries has increased, more Asians have been allowed to settle (10). Some, such as the Vietnamese, are refugees from war-torn countries.

British people are still attracted to Australia. Nurses, for example, are recruited to improve the health and welfare of the population (11). They, like all recent immigrants, come by air (12), and the journey is fast and comfortable (13).

10 Origin of the Australian population, 1985

Born in Australia	79%
Born overseas	21%
of these, UK and Ireland	38%
Continental Europe	36%
Asia	15%
New Zealand	6%
Others	5%

11 Attracting nurses to Australia

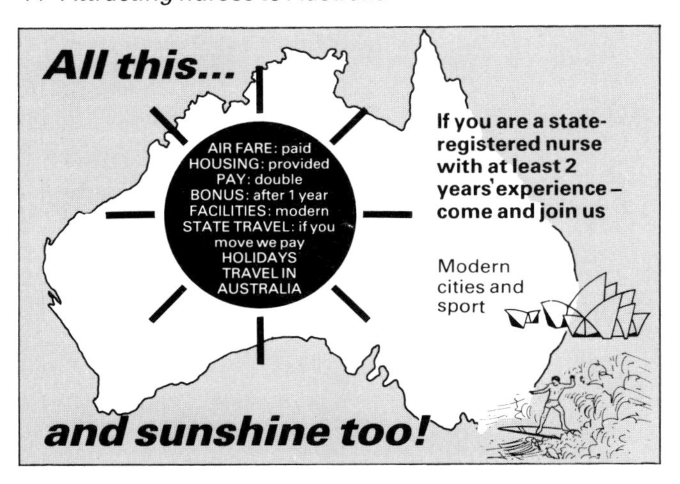

12 Jumbo jet over Sydney

13 London–Sydney flight details

From	Departure time	To	Arrival time (local time)
London	21.45 Monday	Bahrain	06.05 Tuesday
Bahrain	07.15 Tuesday	Singapore	19.35 Tuesday
Singapore	20.40 Tuesday	Sydney	06.30 Wednesday

Note: Sydney local time is 10 hours ahead of Greenwich Mean Time.

> *INTERNATIONAL MIGRATION*
>
> There are many reasons why people migrate from one country to another. Ask for the worksheet.

FOLLOW-UP WORK *(continued)*

3 Mark onto your outline map of question 1 the route taken by the jumbo jet.
4 'Australia is "closer" to Britain today than in the past.' What do you think is meant by this?
5 What have been the main reasons why Australia has wanted immigrants?
6 Migration is the result of two forces, expulsion from one place and attraction to another. These are often called *push* and *pull* factors.
What have been the push and pull factors for each of these groups of people:
(a) British arrivals in the first sixty-five years,
(b) Chinese in the 1850s,
(c) Italians and Greeks in the 1950s,
(d) Vietnamese in the 1970s,
(e) British nurses in the 1980s?
7 List the pull factors shown in the poster (11) under these headings:
social/economic/environmental
8 Explain why Australia wants immigrants with job skills, education, aged 20–34, in good health and with close relatives there.

The dry continent

Australia is the driest continent in the world. If all the rain which falls in one year was evened out over the whole continent, everywhere would receive 470 millimetres. The other continents are much wetter, as is shown in table (14).

14 Average rainfall and evaporation

Continent	*Annual rainfall*	*Evaporation*
South America	1350 mm	64%
North America	670 mm	60%
Africa	670 mm	76%
Asia	610 mm	65%
Europe	600 mm	60%
Australia	470 mm	88%

The main reason Australia is dry is because of its position. Air rises at the Equator and heavy rain falls. The air moves southwards and falls back to the surface over Australia as very dry air. Surface winds bring rain to parts of Australia. This is shown on map (15).

Most of the country is low and flat. The main highland area is the Great Dividing Range which lies close to the east coast. Trade winds from over the Pacific Ocean bring rain to the east coast and to the highlands. By the time the air has passed over the highlands and moved into the interior of Australia, it has become dry.

Australia lies between latitudes 10°S and 44°S, where it is very hot in summer. The heat quickly evaporates most of the rain which falls so there is very little water for crops, animals or people.

Photograph (16) shows a common sight during a drought in New South Wales. The earth is powder-dry, with dead sheep and not a blade of grass to be seen.

15 Climate

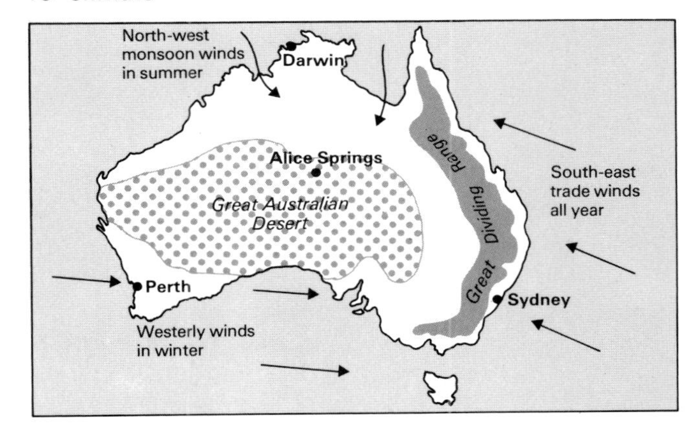

16 Drought scene

> *DROUGHT*
>
> Continuous dry weather. Distress is caused when drought occurs in areas which normally have adequate rainfall.
> Australia's worst drought was in the 1890s when 50 million sheep died.

FOLLOW-UP WORK

1 Link each of the four settlements on map (15) to each climate graph shown in (17). Give reasons for your decisions. Remember that December, January and February are summer months in Australia.

17 Settlements' climate graphs

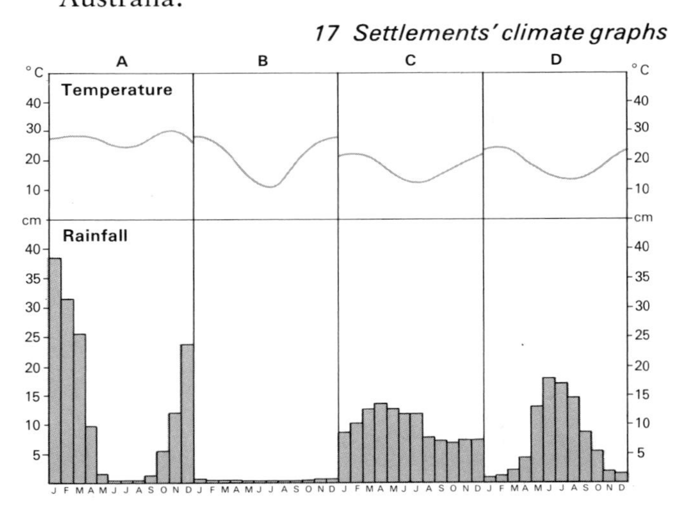

2 Study photograph (16). What does it tell you about rainfall in the interior of Australia? Draw a sketch based on the photograph.
3 How much of Australia is desert?
4 Which winds bring rain to
 (a) the east coast,
 (b) the north coast,
 (c) the south-west coast?
5 Find the dry continent on the photograph of the Pacific world on page 1.

Raising sheep in the dry continent

Mark Wilson is 14 years old and goes to boarding school in Sydney. In December, at the start of the summer holidays, he returns home to his father's sheep station near Menindee. On a Monday Mark caught the 15.15 train to Broken Hill. The journey is 1124 kilometres over the Blue Mountains and across the interior plains. You can study his route on map (18).

As the train descended the western slopes of the highlands, Mark looked out over the lands that the early settlers called the Riverina. These are rich farming lands with deep soils and 500 millimetres of rainfall each year. Wheat is the main crop and Mark could see the early summer harvest taking place. Corriedale sheep are raised here for their lambs. A typical farm of 400 hectares has 200 hectares under wheat and 200 hectares under pasture for grazing 1000 breeding sheep.

After a comfortable night in the air-conditioned train, Mark arrived at Broken Hill at 09.35 on Tuesday. Mark's mother picked him up by jeep at the railway station. They stocked up with food in the town and bought parts for one of the sheep station water pumps.

The two-hour drive to the homestead gave Mark a chance to tell his mother about school in Sydney. He had been on a trip to the wool auctions and seen his father's wool taken by wool buyers from Japan.

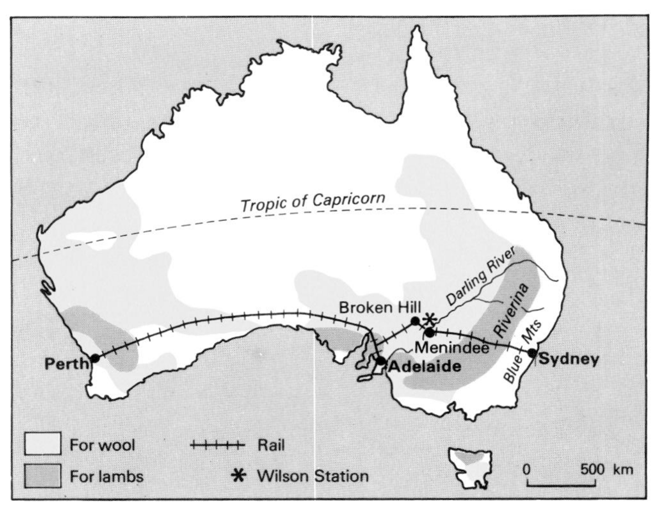

18 Sheep-raising areas

He had wanted to stay with friends in Sydney and spend his days surfing on Bondi Beach, but his father had insisted he came home to help on the station. When Mark arrived at the homestead, he relaxed on the giant veranda and looked out over the plains to the horizon. Mr Wilson told him that there had been rain and that he had stocked up to the maximum 6000 Merino sheep on his 24 000 hectares. Photograph (19) shows a mob of sheep on a good growth of pasture.

Mr Wilson said that when he was a boy, he helped his father on a Welsh hill farm, where they kept 600 sheep on 200 hectares.

19 Sheep at a borehole

The next day Mark went up with his father in the light aircraft. Mark had a map of the station (20) and could easily see its layout as they followed the fifty-kilometre fence.

As they flew over the central paddocks, Mark waved to one of the station hands moving the sheep between paddocks, helped by a kelpie sheepdog. They soon landed at the western paddock, the driest on the station. They cleared a water trough of sand which had blown into it in the last few days, and repaired the pump. Then they were back in the air, following the northern boundary fence. In the north-east paddock they spotted a small group of what looked like dead and crippled sheep. Mr Wilson knew that this was the work of either dingoes that had got through the state dingo fence, or blow-flies.

On landing, they found worms eating the sheep's flesh. Blow-flies had laid eggs on this isolated flock. Blow-fly larvae feed on moist dirty wool at the rear of the sheep. Mr Wilson had removed the tails and rear-end wool of these sheep and had dipped them in a tank of toxic solutions but his efforts had not saved the sheep.

Back at the homestead the family discussed their plans for the year. Lambing would take place in April and May, when the burning summer temperatures of over 35 °C were over. The lambs thrive in the autumn when daytime temperatures are around 17 °C.

The shearing gang had been hired for July. Mr Wilson liked shearing to take place in winter because the sheep needed their wool in the summer to protect them from the heat. A gang of ten men would shear the sheep in a week. When the gang left, Mr Wilson and his two men would finish sorting the wool, press it into bales and take it to the railway at Broken Hill. Mark likes throwing the large fleeces onto the wool table, as in photograph (21).

21 Mark sorts the wool

If the blow-fly damage was not too bad, Mr Wilson hoped to sell 5000 fleeces that year. The wool would go to Sydney because the rail charges were lower than to Adelaide.

Mark spent a hard-working holiday on the station. The sheep were sprayed against another attack of blow-fly. The pastures were treated with fertilizer. The waterholes and boreholes were checked every few days.

WESTERN AND CENTRAL PADDOCKS

Sand soil. Easily blown away. Shrubland vegetation easily damaged by overgrazing. Much bare ground.

EASTERN PADDOCKS

Alluvial clay soil of the river flood plain. Cracks when dry. Good grazing on grassland following rain. Can be irrigated. Deep hollows can be dug or earth dams built to collect rainwater.

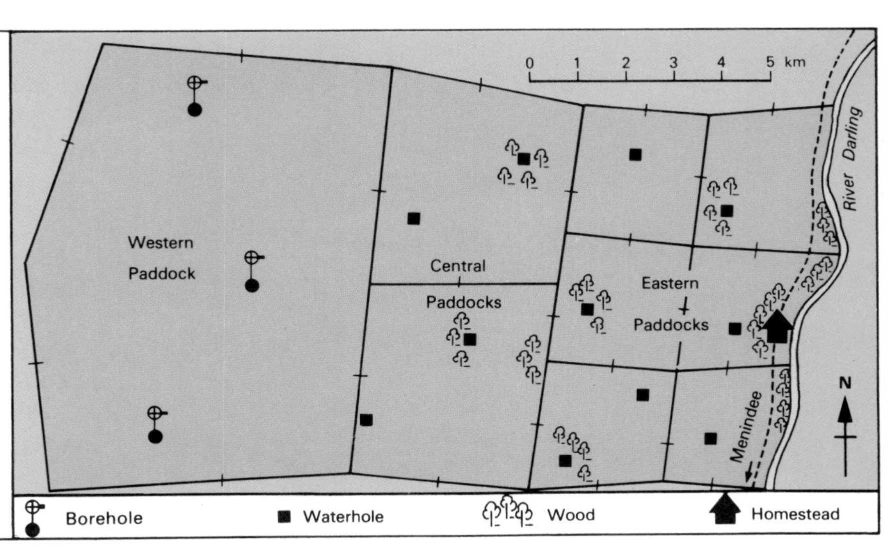

20 Wilson Station, Menindee, New South Wales

Drought on the station

Mark Wilson has a map which shows that his sheep station has an average of 250 millimetres of rainfall a year. Mark knows that in some years the rain does not come. Mr Wilson has to move his sheep to the eastern paddocks but the grass around the waterholes quickly disappears (22).

FOLLOW-UP WORK

1 Piping water from the river

Mr Wilson has borrowed money for pumps, a water tower, pipelines and drinking troughs. Copy the map of the station (20) and mark the position of one 10-kilometre length of pipeline or two 5-kilometre lengths, from the river to the paddocks. Mark the position of ten drinking troughs.

2 Emergency action

The drought continued for another year. Which of the following courses of action would you take? Say why.

(a) Buy huge amounts of extra feed from the wholesalers in Broken Hill.
(b) Sell the sheep that you cannot feed, as most farmers in the west are already doing.
(c) Send sheep to farms further east and pay for them to be fed on irrigated pastures until conditions improve on the station.

22 Sheep at a waterhole

3 Difficult decisions

Although the price for wool has remained steady, Mr Wilson has had less wool to sell because of the drought. The cost of fuel and transport, labour, fertilizers and the interest on his loan are all high. He is considering the following courses of action. Which one would you suggest? Say why.

(a) Lay off one of the two workers.
(b) Cut down on the use of fertilizer.
(c) Stop the usual practice of buying high-quality rams each year.
(d) Sell the light aircraft.
(e) Borrow more money.

> *EXTENSIVE PASTORAL FARMING*
>
> Pastoral farming is the rearing of animals. Extensive farming has a small input of labour and low output per hectare from large areas of land. Low output often results from harsh physical conditions as well as low human and economic inputs.

4 Features of the farm

(a) How many hectares are needed to raise one sheep on the sheep station?
(b) How many sheep can be raised on one hectare on
  (i) a typical farm in the Riverina,
  (ii) a Welsh hill farm?
(c) Why does Mr Wilson keep sheep for their wool and not for the sale of lambs?
(d) Why do only a few men work on such a large sheep station?
(e) Why are the eastern paddocks the best on the station?
(f) How does the size and location of the sheep station help to explain
  (i) why Mark Wilson goes to boarding school,
  (ii) why Mr Wilson has a light aircraft,
  (iii) why transport costs are high,
  (iv) why the workers live on the station?
(g) What are the three different sources of water which Mr Wilson can use on the sheep station?

> *THE FARMING SYSTEM*
>
> Farming is a system with inputs, processes and outputs. Ask for the farm system sheet. Mark into the spaces on the sheet all the details you can obtain from your study of Wilson's sheep station. Write exact information if it is available. You may write *high*, *low* or *nil* in some boxes. The completed sheet can be used to compare the many different types of farming included in this book.

Storing water

Ord River Project

Water is in short supply over large areas of Australia. We have seen that 88 per cent of the rainfall evaporates. Half the remaining water sinks into the ground, and the rest flows across the surface of the land in streams and rivers.

In northern Australia there is rain in summer and the rest of the year is dry. This is shown in the rainfall statistics for Wyndham (23).

24 Lake Argyle

23 Rainfall statistics for Wyndham

Jan	*Feb*	*Mar*	*Apr*	*May*	*Jun*	*Jul*	*Aug*	*Sept*	*Oct*	*Nov*	*Dec*	*Total mm*
200	160	140	50	10	2	1	2	10	30	70	140	815

Great efforts are made to collect, store and carefully use the summer rainfall. Photograph (24) shows Lake Argyle which was made in 1972 by building a dam across the River Ord in northern Australia. The location of the project is shown on maps (25) and (26). The water irrigates the land for sugar-cane and other tropical crops. Water is also used to provide good grazing land for beef cattle, which dramatically improves the cattle quality.

Cattle ranches are huge unfenced areas of coarse tropical grassland. A typical ranch has a herd of 70 000 Shorthorns. Each animal needs twenty hectares of land to survive. The animals are mustered once a year, before the dry season begins. The young stock are branded and the 4- and 5-year-old animals are trucked to the meatworks at Wyndham, as in photograph (27). The animals suffer from pests and diseases and many die near the end of the dry season. The meat from these half-wild animals is very poor and is used to make beefburgers for the American market. In the Ord River valley, in contrast, cattle graze on irrigated pastures, few die, they are ready for the meatworks in three years, and give good-quality meat.

The spread of cattle-ranching in northern Australia came with the discovery of underground supplies of water from rock basins, called artesian basins, shown on map (28). The first water was brought to the surface in 1879, and now there are 18 000 boreholes providing water for cattle.

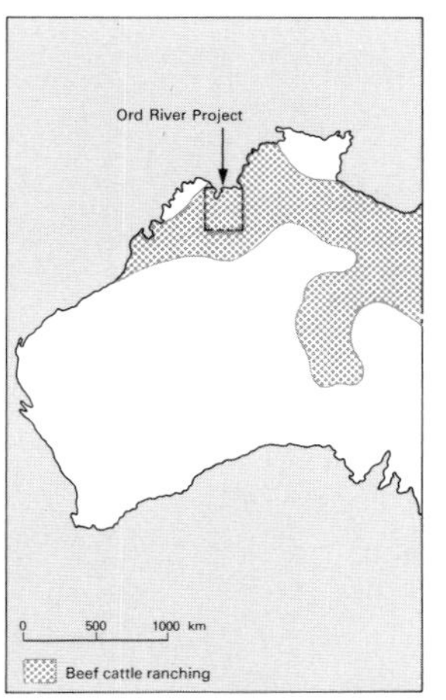

25 Location of Ord River Project

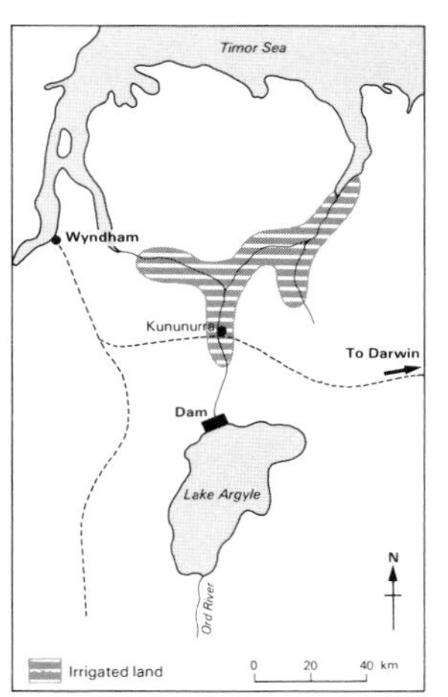

26 Ord River Project

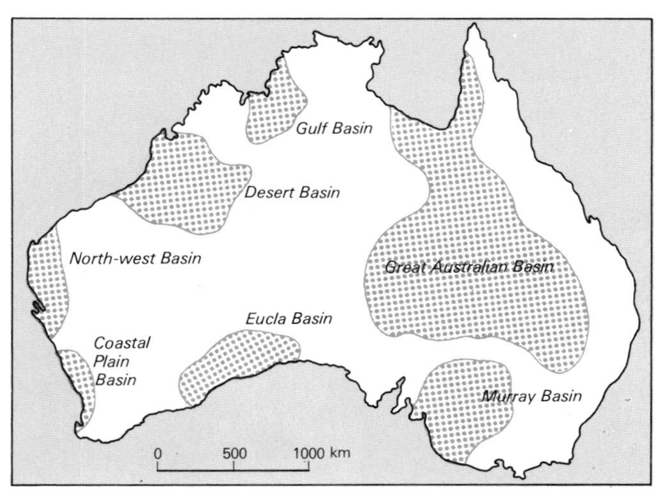

28 Artesian basins

27 Trucking cattle to the meatworks

The Snowy Mountains Scheme

The south-east coast of Australia has rain every month, as you can see from the rainfall statistics for Sydney (29).

Inland from the Great Dividing Range, there is less rain in what is called the rainshadow area. You saw these changes on Mark Wilson's journey from Sydney to Broken Hill.

The largest water storing scheme in Australia is in the Snowy Mountains. Its aim is to divert water from the east of the mountains, where it is wet, to the west of the mountains, where it is dry. The scheme was begun in 1949 and completed in 1974.

In 1957, a dam was built across the River Eucumbene to make Lake Eucumbene, shown in photograph (30). A tunnel was bored through the mountains, to take water to Tumut River, and so into the dry plains.

30 Lake Eucumbene

29 Rainfall statistics for Sydney

Jan	*Feb*	*Mar*	*Apr*	*May*	*Jun*	*Jul*	*Aug*	*Sept*	*Oct*	*Nov*	*Dec*	*Total mm*
89	102	127	135	127	117	117	76	74	71	74	74	1183

Now study the maps (31) and (32). A dam was built on Snowy River to make the Island Bend Reservoir, and a second tunnel was cut through the mountains to take water to Murray River. A second dam lower down Snowy River made Lake Jindabyne. Water is taken from this lake to Island Bend Reservoir when extra water supplies are needed.

A third tunnel from Island Bend Reservoir to Lake Eucumbene links the two sections of the scheme, and water can be sent in either direction as needed.

As the water passes through the tunnels, it drops 800 metres and generates electricity at seven power stations. This electricity is used in the cities of Sydney, Canberra and Melbourne. Photograph (33) shows the Tumut 1 power station which is 365 metres underground.

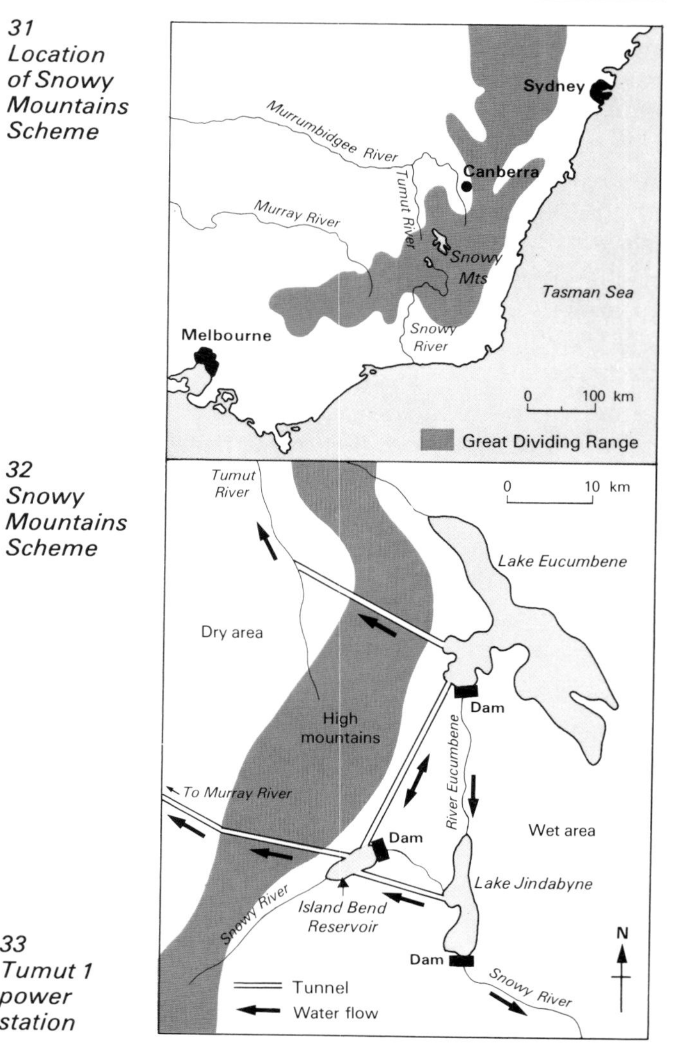

31 Location of Snowy Mountains Scheme

32 Snowy Mountains Scheme

◀ *33 Tumut 1 power station*

Farmers in the interior plains now get reliable water supplies. The land that the Rivers Murray and Murrumbidgee can irrigate has been increased by over a quarter. Photograph (34) shows irrigated vineyards and orchards beside the Murray River. Notice the regular pattern of fields and farm buildings.

The roads which were made by the construction gangs in the Snowy Mountains are now used by holidaymakers. The lakes not only store water for making electricity and providing irrigation but also give pleasure to thousands of visitors each year.

> *MULTI-PURPOSE SCHEME*
>
> The Snowy Mountains Scheme is a multi-purpose scheme. This means the project has many uses which have benefits for different groups of people.

FOLLOW-UP WORK

1 Use the rainfall statistics in table (23) to draw a bar graph of the monthly rainfall in the Ord River valley. Use a scale of 20 mm rainfall to 1 cm of the vertical axis.
2 Copy the cross-section (35) of south-east Australia. Colour the columns in blue to the correct height, using the rainfall statistics beneath the columns.
3 Study the graph you drew for question 1 and the cross-section of question 2. What are the different needs for storing water in the Ord River valley and in the Snowy Mountains?

> *3-D MODEL*
>
> A simple three-dimensional reproduction of the landscape made from paper, card or other material. The length and breadth are to scale but altitude is exaggerated.
> Ask for the Snowy Mountains Scheme model sheet and exercises.

34 Irrigated land by the River Murray

4 Using your knowledge of the Snowy Mountains Scheme and this sketch, explain what is meant by water transfer.

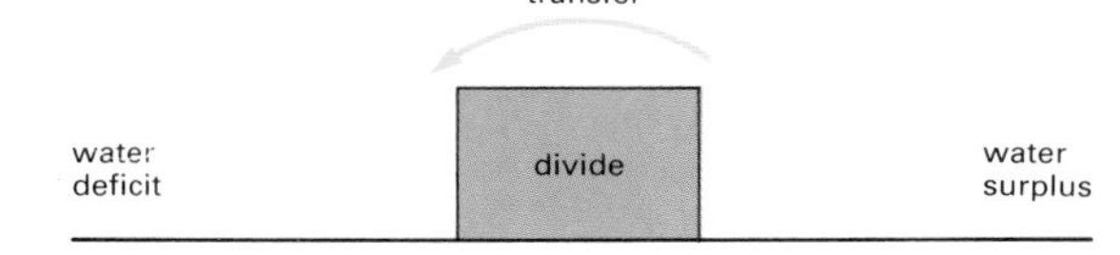

5 How does the cross-section you drew for question 2 show why there is a need for a water transfer scheme?
6 What are the main uses for the Snowy Mountains Scheme?
7 How does the location of the Ord River Project help to explain why it has fewer uses?
8 Study photograph (34). In what ways is the farming landscape in the foreground different from that in the sheep-rearing areas (pages 10–12)?

TROUBLE IN TASMANIA

People are in conflict over the use of parts of the island state of Tasmania for building dams and making reservoirs. Ask for details.

35 Cross-section of south-east Australia

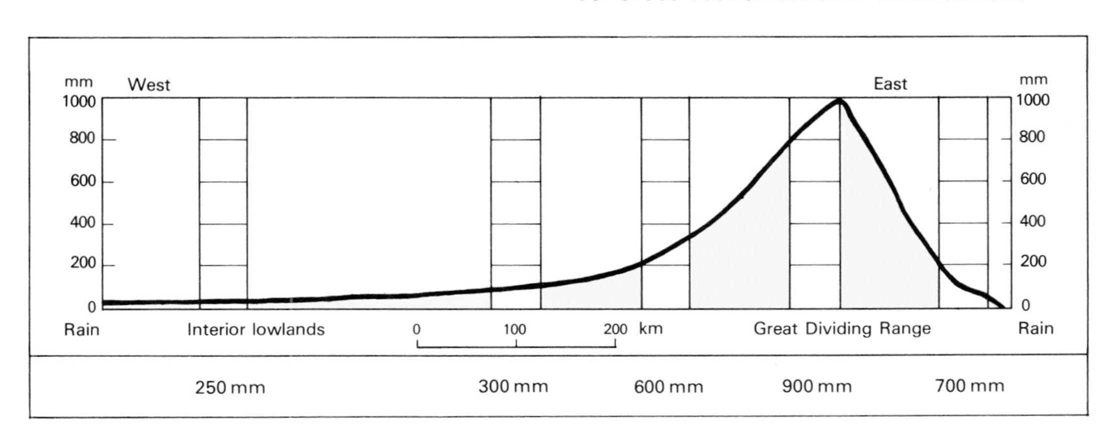

Mineral resources and industry

Australia is rich in mineral resources. The ancient igneous rocks in the west of Australia hold a vast reserve of metallic minerals including iron ore, nickel, zinc, lead and gold. Coal is found in the sedimentary strata in the east of the country (36).

Mining was of little importance until the 1960s when a combination of factors brought rapid developments.

- Exploration revealed vast reserves of high-grade iron ore in Western Australia and great thicknesses of coal in Queensland and New South Wales.
- The Australian government, having banned iron ore exports in 1938 to preserve what it thought were limited resources, allowed exports from 1960. The government of Western Australia issued leases to big development companies from 1961.
- Japan began what became a spectacular industrial growth based upon imported raw materials. Australia provided much of the coal and iron ore.
- A revolution in sea transport resulted in bulk-carrier ships which could carry bulk cargoes of low-value minerals long distances at low cost.
- Advances in mechanisation resulted in massive opencast mining machinery and transport equipment (37).

36 Iron ore and coal sites

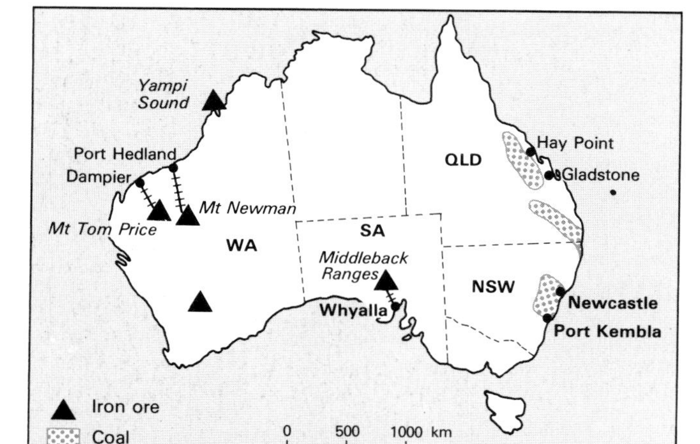

RESOURCES

These are the things which are available in the world for people to use.
Renewable resources such as crops and trees can be produced and used time and time again.
Non-renewable (or finite) resources such as minerals, once used cannot be replaced.

37 Iron ore mining, Mount Newman

Coal output continued to rise because increases in the price for oil in the 1970s caused an increased demand for low-priced coal for energy. Iron ore output rose as more countries such as Taiwan and Korea based new steel industries on imported coal and iron ore. Even countries such as the UK with their own supplies of coal and iron ore found it cheaper to buy raw materials from Australia. The results are seen in table (38).

38 Coal and iron ore production

Coal			
	Production Million tonnes	*Exports (1987) Total 97m tonnes Main markets*	
1960	23	Japan	45%
1965	32	South Korea	8%
1970	50	Taiwan	6%
1975	68	Netherlands	6%
1980	98	France	4%
1985	129	Denmark	4%
1987	175	UK	3%
		Others	24%
Iron ore			
	Production Million tonnes	*Exports (1987) Total 73m tonnes Main markets*	
1960	5	Japan	55%
1965	7	China	10%
1970	51	South Korea	7%
1975	98	West Germany	6%
1980	88	UK	5%
1985	93	France	4%
1987	100	Taiwan	4%
		Others	9%

39 Port Kembla

The steel industry in Australia Australia produces 6 million tonnes of steel each year. There are three tidewater locations on the south and east coasts at Port Kembla, Newcastle and Whyalla which use Australian coal and iron ore (36). A 'mini' steelworks near Melbourne produces 250 000 tonnes of steel a year in an electric furnace using scrap.

The problem for the steel industry is the cost of transporting coal and iron ore long distances. Iron ore from Port Hedland is unloaded at Port Kembla (39). The same ships are loaded with coal, from local collieries, for transport to Japan and South Korea before returning to Port Hedland. In this way cargo is carried on two legs of a triangle of trade which reduces the cost of transport for both the iron ore and the coal.

Steel to make cars The car industry is the most important user of steel. There are car works in Adelaide (40), Geelong, Sydney and Melbourne. Only 300 000 cars are made, mainly for Australia and New Zealand. The main problems are the small home market and competition from Japan.

40 Car assembly works in Adelaide

FOLLOW-UP WORK

1 Port Kembla is a large integrated steelworks with a capacity of 5.5 million tonnes of steel each year. Study map (36), photo (39) and table (41). Name four advantages of building a steelworks at Port Kembla.
2 Copy map (36). Mark onto the map the sea routes which bulk-carriers follow carrying iron ore and coal to the three steelworks. Use the information provided in table (41). Draw lines in *red* for iron ore and *green* for coal.
3 If the bulk-carriers travel 500 kilometres each day, how long will a ship be at sea carrying iron ore from Port Hedland to Port Kembla?
4 Trace a map from your atlas which shows Australia and Japan. Mark on your map the triangle of trade for a ship from Port Hedland to Port Kembla to Tokyo, and back to Port Hedland. Explain why this provides cheaper transport than separate *return* trips between Port Hedland and Port Kembla, and Port Kembla and Tokyo.
5 Suggest reasons why a steelworks has not been built at Port Hedland.
6 Name three advantages for building car assembly works in Melbourne and Adelaide.

TOPOLOGICAL WORLD MAP

Countries and continents are shown in roughly their correct location but they are drawn with a regular shape and their size is proportional to the data being used. They can be used to show the size of population or the amount of mineral resources, for example. Ask for the topological map of world coal resources.

41 Iron and steel works

Iron and steelworks	*Location*	*Iron ore supplies*	*Coal supplies*
Port Kembla	85 km south of Sydney	Port Hedland, Yampi Sound and Whyalla	Local collieries
Newcastle	170 km north of Sydney	Port Hedland, Yampi Sound and Whyalla	Local collieries
Whyalla	Spencer Gulf	Middleback Ranges 50 km rail link	Port Kembla, Newcastle and Gladstone

Cities

Australia is a big country with a small population. If its 16 million people were evenly spread over the land, there would be two people on each square kilometre. Map (42) shows that the population is not evenly spread. Most Australians live near the sea between Brisbane in Queensland and Adelaide in South Australia.

One hundred years ago, Australia was a farming country with 2 million people. Since then, small coastal towns have grown into large cities. The state capitals are very important, and over 40 per cent of all Australians live in the two capitals of Sydney and Melbourne. Many reasons for the growth of cities are shown on diagram (43).

42 Spread of population

43 Growth of an Australian city

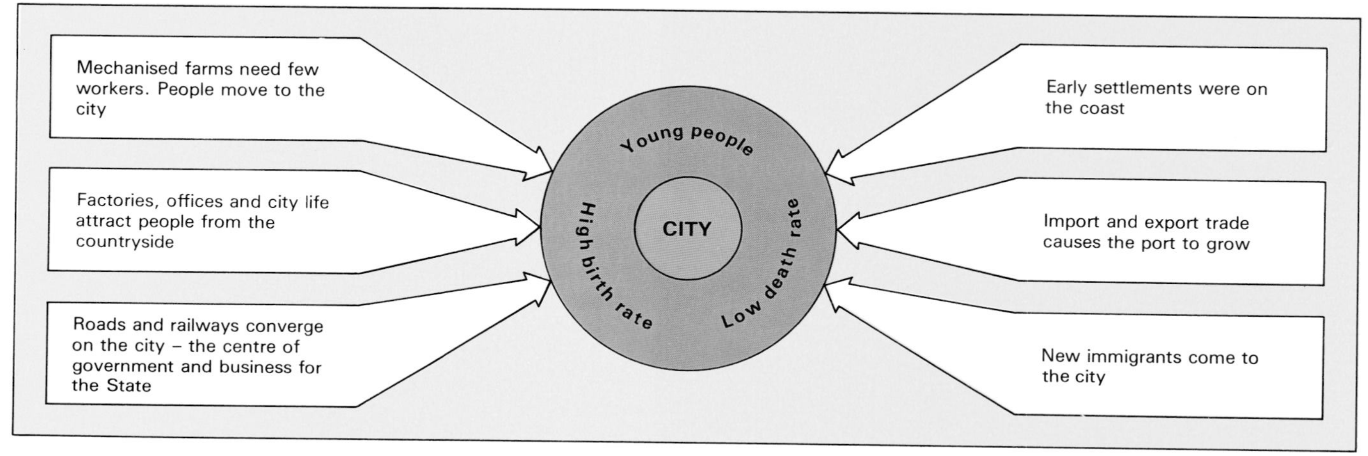

44 Sydney

Sydney

In 1788, Britain planted her first settlement in Australia at Sydney Cove on the deep inlet called Port Jackson. This site was chosen instead of Botany Bay because of its sheltered deep water and freshwater spring. Today more than 3 million people live in Sydney. The original site is covered with office blocks and overlooked by Sydney Harbour Bridge. Sydney is Australia's largest city, its chief port and the most important centre of industry, business and transport. It is the capital city of New South Wales.

Now study the photograph (44) of Sydney. Notice Sydney Harbour Bridge which carries an eight-lane highway and twin-track railway over the Port Jackson inlet. Tall office blocks overlook Sydney Cove where large ships can dock. Sydney Opera House is a clear landmark with a roof like the spinnaker sails of a racing-yacht. In the background is Botany Bay.

Sydney is a busy city. People travel from pleasant housing areas north of Port Jackson, across the Harbour Bridge to offices, shops and factories in the south of the city. At summer weekends, families will be heading for the beaches or out to the parks and camping sites. Study map (45), which shows all the centres of activity in the city.

45 *Sydney*

1 Outer light industry
Modern factories, light engineering

2 Heavy industry
2A Oil refining, cars, rubber, heavy engineering.
2B Oil refining, chemicals, metal, brick and leather works.

3 Inner light industry
Food, clothing, household goods, light engineering. Factories extend along the roads.

4 Botany Bay port
A modern port on reclaimed land. Oil tankers, bulk carriers and container ships berth here.

5 Coast recreation area
Thirty-five surfing beaches including Bondi and Manly. See photograph (46).

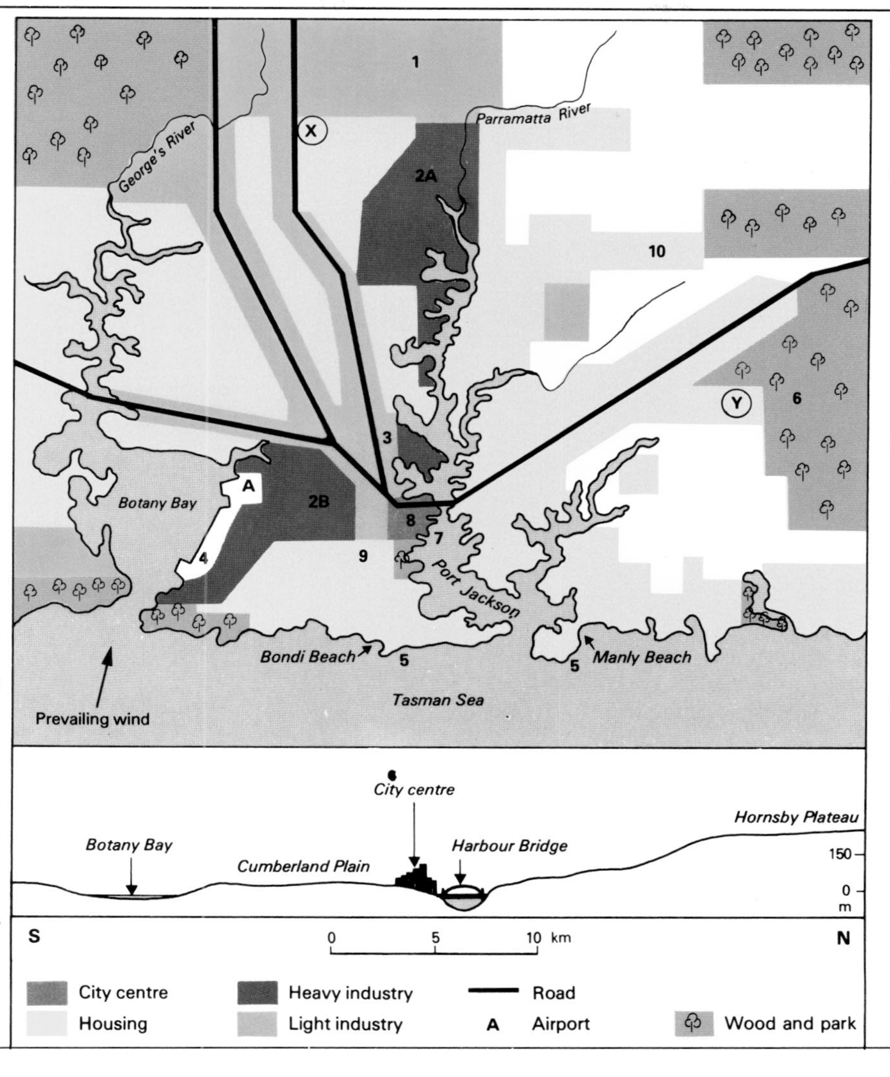

6 Inland recreation area
Nature reserves and national parks.

7 Port Jackson
The original port on the south side of the inlet. Passenger, container and general cargo ships berth here. Imports of oil, coal, timber, cars and machinery. Exports of wool and wheat.

8 Central business district
Offices, banks and government buildings. Shops, restaurants, theatres and cinemas. The opera house. Parks and gardens. Routes converge on the Harbour Bridge.

9 Inner housing area
Nineteenth-century terraced houses and modern blocks of flats.

10 Outer housing areas
Detached bungalows, schools and shops. See photograph (47).

46 *Bondi Beach*

47 *Housing in Sydney suburbs*

FOLLOW-UP WORK

1 There are positive and negative factors which help to explain why people settle in some areas but not others. These are examples:

Positive factors	Negative factors
Warm	Cold
Moist	Dry
Lowland	Mountainous
Accessible	Remote
Fertile soil	Barren land
Mineral resources	Lack of resources
Grassland	Rainforest

The positive factors help to explain why most Australians live in coastal areas in the south and east of the country. Which of the negative factors help to explain why few people live in areas 1, 2 and 3 on map (42)?

2 Copy diagram (48). Using the statistics in table (49), colour each column to show how many people in each state live in the capital. Sydney has been done for you.

3 (a) Which two state capitals have the highest proportion of the state population?
(b) What percentage of Australia's 16 million people live in the six state capitals?
(c) What are the main reasons why such a large proportion of people live in the capital cities? Use diagram (43) on page 18.

4 The Turner family live in Dubbo, a small country town 400 kilometres west of Sydney. Mr Turner has decided to sell his garage business and move into Sydney. He has found work in a car factory but hopes to set up his own engineering works. His wife and elder son have office jobs and his two younger children are at school. What are the advantages of the family moving to Sydney?

5 The Turners intend to buy a block of land in Sydney and build their own home. This will be a detached bungalow and garden like the one in (47). The price of land varies, generally getting cheaper the greater the distance from the city centre. Price also depends upon the pleasantness of the locality and the availability of services such as transport, schools and shops. The Turners have decided to live in a suburb. Plots are for sale at X and Y on map (45).
Which would you choose? Say why.

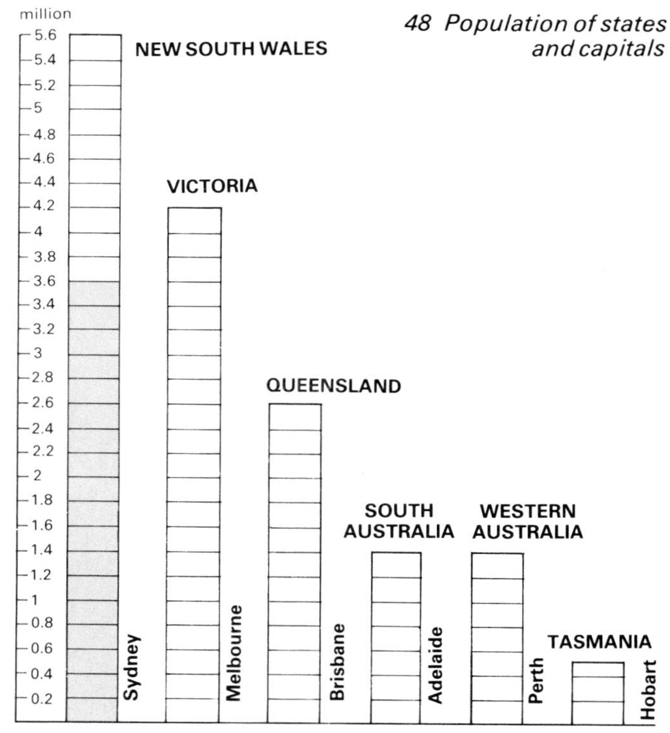

48 Population of states and capitals

As Sydney grew, certain areas developed a particular function such as housing, business and industry. Study these areas on map (45) and answer these questions.

6 Why are offices, shops and places of entertainment located in the city centre?

7 What advantages are there in locating factories (a) near the city centre, (b) along roads, (c) on the outskirts?

8 Suggest reasons why heavy industry and light industry have different locations in the city.

9 (a) Why are the oldest houses near the centre of the city?
(b) Why are the most expensive new houses in the north of Sydney?
(c) Suggest two reasons why housing has spread over a large area.

10 (a) Why was Port Jackson developed before Botany Bay?
(b) What advantages and problems does Botany Bay have as a port?

11 In which parts of the city will there be traffic congestion
(a) on weekdays, (b) at summer weekends?

49 State population living in capital, 1987

	Sydney	*Melbourne*	*Brisbane*	*Adelaide*	*Perth*	*Hobart*
Million	3.6	3.0	1.2	1.0	1.0	0.2
%	64	71	46	72	72	40

Northern Territory 150 000 *Australian Capital Territory* 266 000

URBAN MODELS

It is possible to identify a pattern in the land use of a city which helps us to understand how the city has grown and works. Ask for the information sheet.

Transport

Australia is a big continent and most of its 16 million people live in a few large cities which are hundreds and in some cases thousands of kilometres apart. Transport and communication are vital but costly to provide. Most people own cars as a necessity rather than as a luxury. This is similar to the motorised way of living in the USA and Canada, as is shown in table (50). The roads in the cities and suburbs are very busy.

50 Cars per thousand people, 1985

USA	*Canada*	*Australia*	*UK*	*Japan*	*China*
556	455	435	345	233	0.05

Most main roads and railways were built in the second half of the nineteenth century when Australia consisted of six colonies. Each colony had its own routes radiating from the capital city. These routes were and still remain the arteries for carrying minerals and food products from the hinterland to the coast for export. The most recently built railway lines carry iron ore from the Pilbara district of Western Australia to the coast for export, mainly to Japan (51).

51 The railway network

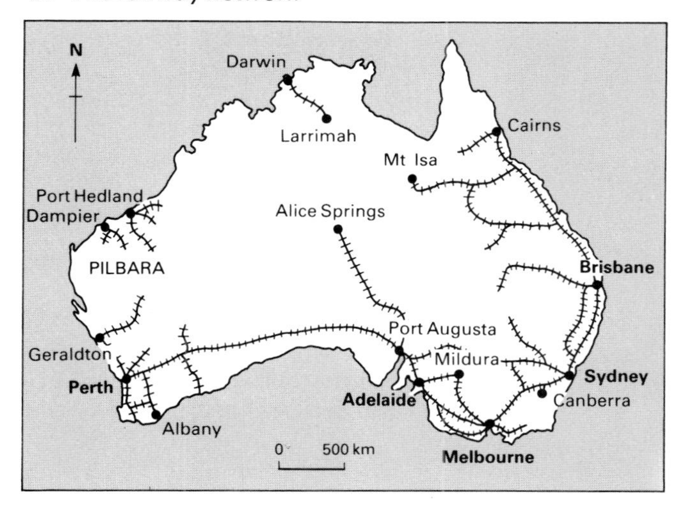

> *TRANSPORT AND COMMUNICATION*
>
> Transport is the movement of people and goods from one place to another by road, rail, sea and air.
> Communication is the transmission of information from one place to another, by telephone, radio, television and newspapers, for example.

> *HINTERLAND*
>
> The land behind a port or seaboard to which it distributes imports and from which it gathers products for export. The term is often used to describe the area of influence of any town or city.

Each state had a different railway gauge. It was only in 1984 that all the mainland capital cities were connected by standard-gauge track. This helps to show that the railways have continued to serve the state and its overseas trade more than trade between states.

The Trans-Australian Railway, linking Adelaide to Perth, was completed in 1917 when the section between Port Augusta and Kalgoorlie was opened to traffic (53). There was a political reason for building the railway because it was promised to Western Australia as an incentive to join the united country, the Commonwealth of Australia, in 1901. The new track helped the development of mining, such as the gold district of Kalgoorlie, and also extended wheat production and pastoral farming into semi-arid areas of the country. The Indian-Pacific is a passenger train which runs three times each week between Sydney and Perth. The train carries 142 passengers, mainly retired people and tourists who want to experience the country in air-conditioned comfort. Your view is from the driver's cab across the barren Nullarbor Plain (52). The railway competes with road transport only in carrying bulk cargoes long distances. Grain, minerals, steel, new cars and containers are the main cargoes.

The aeroplane is the best answer to the problem of distance. Businessmen and tourists often fly from city to city, leaving the long straight roads, such as the Eyre Highway (53, 54) empty of traffic. Changes in travel by rail, car and air are shown in table (55).

52 View from cab of Indian-Pacific Railway

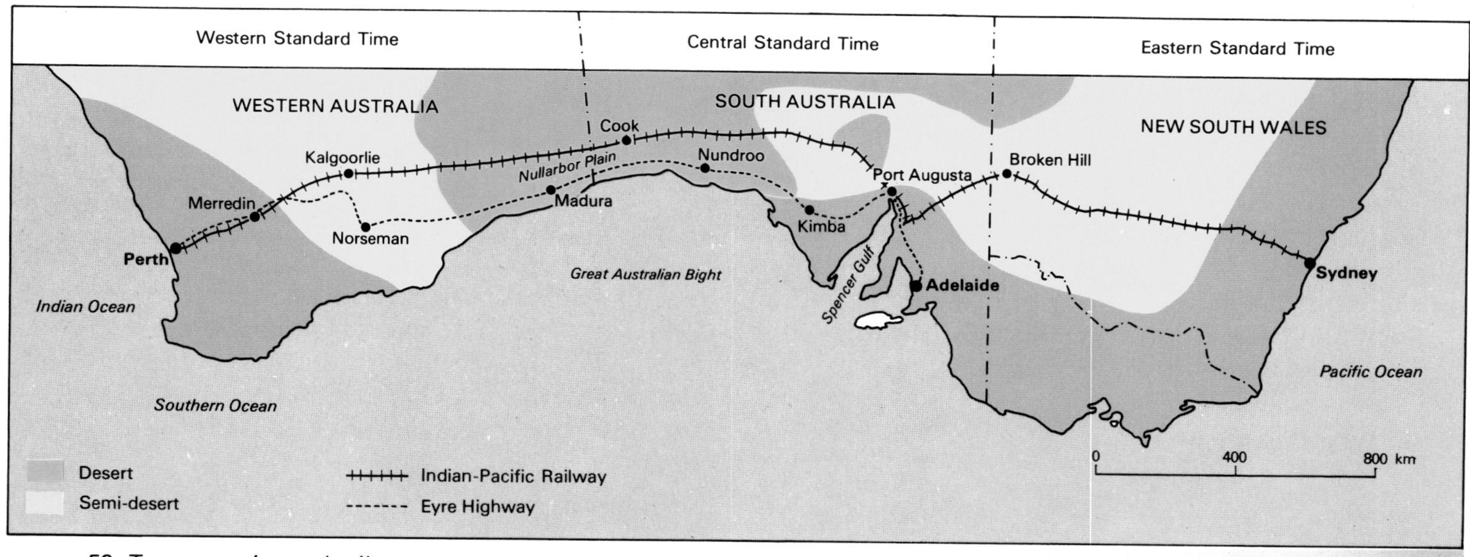

53 Trans-continental railway

FOLLOW-UP WORK

1 Study table (55). Suggest reasons why travel by car and aeroplane has increased whereas rail travel has declined.

55 Passenger journeys (millions)

Year	*By rail*	*By air*	*Cars on the road*
1966	460	3.0	3.0
1985	403	10.6	6.8

2 Study map (53) and train timetable (56).
  (a) What are the advantages of a rail link between Sydney and Perth? Mention the two cities and the area that the railway crosses.
  (b) Which states do you travel through on this journey?
  (c) How many hours does the journey take?
  (d) The air flight from Sydney to Perth takes five hours. How does this help to explain the importance of air flight for passengers living in such a big country?

56 Journey times, Sydney to Perth

Sydney	Mon	15.15	0 km	
Broken Hill	Tue	09.35	1124 km	(put watches back 30 mins)
Port Augusta	Tue	18.30	1614 km	
Cook	Wed	08.25	2436 km	(put watches back 90 mins)
Kalgoorlie	Wed	19.45	3304 km	
Perth	Thur	07.00	3961 km	

3 Study the map of the railway network (51).
  (a) Why are most railways in the south and east of the country?
  (b) Why are there many straight lines from the coast to the interior?

54 Eyre Highway, east of Norseman

  c) Why are the lines in the east of the country linked together along the coast?
  (d) Why does the trans-continental line run west to east and *not* north to south?

4 Suggest some political, social and economic reasons for building railways in Australia.

5 Australia is divided into three time zones (53). Time is the same within each zone.
  (a) What are the names of the three time zones?
  (b) Why are watches put back when you travel west (56)?
  (c) When it is 7.00 a.m. in Perth, what time is it in Sydney?

6 'Australians have conquered the distances between cities but not the land itself.' What does this statement mean?

AUSTRALIA: TIME AND DISTANCE

Ask for the worksheet.

> *TRANSPORT NETWORK*
>
> A pattern of interconnected lines of transport. A developed network has a large number of interconnections allowing goods and people to move easily between places.

Trade with the world

Photograph (57) shows a container ship leaving the busy port of Sydney. Products from Australia's farms and mines are the main cargoes.

Britain was Australia's main trading partner until the Second World War. Since then, Australia has found new markets for her products in countries of the Pacific world.

Study tables (58)–(61) which show the items of trade and main trading partners in 1985.

FOLLOW-UP WORK

1 Draw pie graphs to show Australian exports and imports, using the percentages from tables (58) and (60).
2 Draw simple bar graphs to show Australia's major trading partners and the value of their trade. Use the data shown in tables (59) and (61).
3 Mark Australia's main trading partners on an outline map of the world. Add coloured arrows to show the amount and the direction of flow of goods between each country and Australia.
4 Why does Australia need to trade?
5 Suggest reasons why Britain is no longer Australia's main trading partner.
6 (a) Which two countries are Australia's main trading partners today?
(b) Suggest reasons for the close trading links between Australia and Japan.
7 (a) Which group of exports, shown in table (58), would not have been important before the Second World War?
(b) Which group of imports, shown in table (60), would not have been important before the Second World War?
8 Explain why New Zealand buys manufactured goods from Australia.

57 Container ship leaves Sydney

TOPIC FOR DISCUSSION

Australia relies too much on the export of its natural resources. It should have developed export industries as Japan, Singapore, Taiwan and Hong Kong have done.

58 Exports (by value)

36%	*Farm products* mainly wheat, wool, meat, sugar and dairy products
19%	*Manufactured goods* including steel, machines, cars, textiles and chemicals
41%	*Minerals* including iron ore, coal and bauxite
4%	*Others*

59 Main markets for these exports

Japan	27%
USA	12%
New Zealand	5%
UK	4%
West Germany	3%
Singapore	3%
Hong Kong	3%
USSR	3%
France	2%
Malaysia	2%

60 Imports (by value)

84%	*Manufactured goods* including machines, vehicles, textiles, electrical goods and chemicals
10%	*Materials for industry* including oil, timber and rubber
6%	*Farm products* including coffee, tea and cocoa

61 Main suppliers of these imports

USA	23%
Japan	22%
UK	7%
West Germany	6%
New Zealand	4%
Italy	3%
Singapore	3%
Hong Kong	2%
Saudi Arabia	2%
Canada	2%

New Zealand

1 Mountains and sea

Islands in the South Pacific

Ten million years ago, the waters of the Pacific Ocean were disturbed by great earthquakes, and the rocks of the sea-bed rose into the air. Two large islands and many small ones were formed, with mountain peaks over 3000 metres above the waves (1). New Zealand as we know it today was born, 1500 kilometres south-east of Australia. Eighty million years ago the land that is now New Zealand was attached to Australia. Then it split and moved away on a moving plate of the earth's crust.

New Zealand lies above the line where two plates meet. You can make a model which shows why there are active volcanoes (2) and why earthquakes are a regular occurrence (3). Ask for the model sheet and instructions.

New Zealand is about the same size as Britain. The two main islands are long and narrow with hills and mountains (4). Unlike Australia, New Zealand is wet. Westerly winds bring heavy rain to western slopes. Trade winds blow across North Island in summer, bringing rain from the east.

Thick forest once covered New Zealand. Giant kauri pines (5) thrived in the warmth and plentiful rainfall of North Island. Beech forest grew on the western slopes of South Island. Only the ice- and snow-covered mountain peaks had no trees.

PLATES

The large blocks into which the earth's crust is divided. They move on top of the hot and sometimes molten mantle. Mountains, earthquakes and volcanoes occur where the leading edge of two plates push against each other.

3 Newspaper report

Quake causes havoc in New Zealand

2 March 1987

A state of emergency was declared in parts of New Zealand's North Island after an earthquake measuring 6.5 on the Richter scale hit the coastal area of the Bay of Plenty at 1.36 p.m. yesterday. One witness said 'the earth rolled like the sea' and others said homes and offices shook for more than thirty seconds.

About 50 000 people live in the affected area, mostly rolling farmland and forest. The worst-hit town was Whakatane where most of the houses were damaged. Forestry workers were injured by falling trees and motorists were hurt in landslides. A fissure two kilometres long sliced through farmland. The crack, several metres deep, missed houses by only metres but carried away driveways, milking sheds, power lines and bridges.

One hundred aftershocks measuring 4.5 on the Richter scale continued for more than 24 hours after the main event. One person has died, several more are seriously injured and there are many minor injuries.

2 Volcanoes (left)

4 Climate (below)

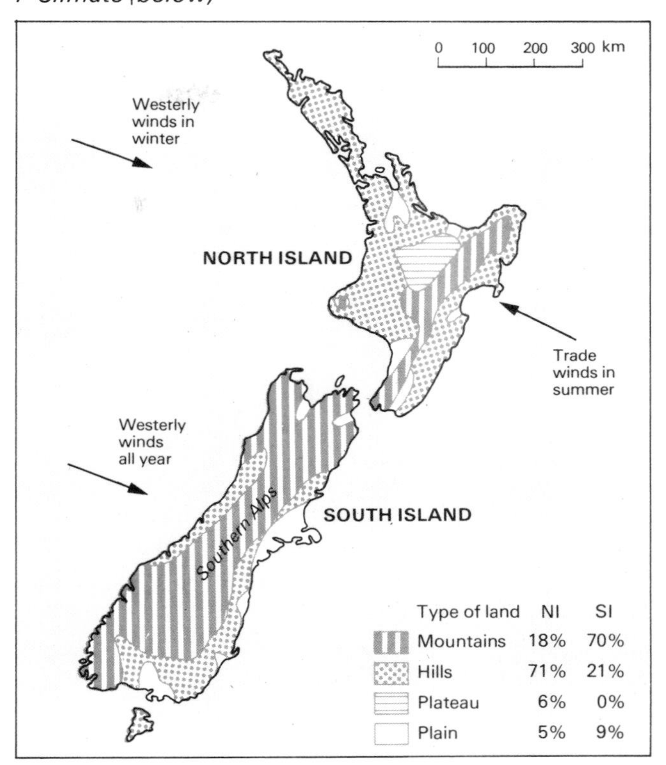

On the drier plains to the east of the Southern Alps there was an open woodland with tussock grasses.

FOLLOW-UP WORK

1 Study the model and use it to answer these questions.
   (a) Which two plates meet in the vicinity of New Zealand?
   (b) Which plate is moving downwards
      (i) north of New Zealand,
      (ii) south of New Zealand?
   (c) How does the model help to explain the occurrence of
      (i) ranges of mountains along the length of both islands,
      (ii) regular earthquakes,
      (iii) a line of volcanoes,
      (iv) a deep ocean trench?
2 Read the newspaper article (3).
   (a) Why was the earthquake in the Bay of Plenty and not further west in Auckland, for example? (Use an atlas and your model.)
   (b) What were the main effects of the earthquake?
   (c) Suggest reasons why there was little loss of life as a result of this big earthquake.
3 Draw pie graphs to show the amount of mountain, hill, plateau and plain on each island. Use the percentages from map (4).
   What do the pie graphs tell you about the land of New Zealand?
4 Trace map (4). With the help of an atlas, mark the following onto the map:
   Southern Alps; Mount Cook; Canterbury Plains; Volcanic Plateau: Mount Ruapehu; Tararua Range.
   In what direction do the mountain ranges lie?
5 How does the direction of the mountain ranges help to explain why the west side of South Island is wetter than the east?
6 Why is North Island warmer than South Island?

5 Kauri pines

Moahunters, Maoris and Europeans

The first people to live in New Zealand hunted a large flightless bird, called the moa. The moa lived in the open woodlands and tussock grasslands of South Island. Photograph (6) was posed to show what a moa hunt was like hundreds of years ago. As the Moahunters increased in number, the number of moas quickly fell. The last moas were caught by setting fire to the woodlands and grass to scare the birds into the open. By the thirteenth century, the number of Moahunters was 10 000 but the moa was extinct.

Maoris landed in New Zealand from other islands in the Pacific during the thirteenth and fourteenth centuries. The Moahunters died out during this time.

The Maoris grew root crops, including sweet potatoes and yams. They were shifting cultivators. A patch of forest was cleared and the land cultivated with a ko (7). When the land began to lose its fertility, they cleared another patch of forest. Like the Moahunters, the Maoris ate fern-roots, berries, birds and fish. They also ate dog, rat and sometimes human flesh.

Map (8) shows where the Moahunters and Maoris lived.

6 Moa hunt

7 Maori land cultivation

8 Where the Moahunters and Maoris lived

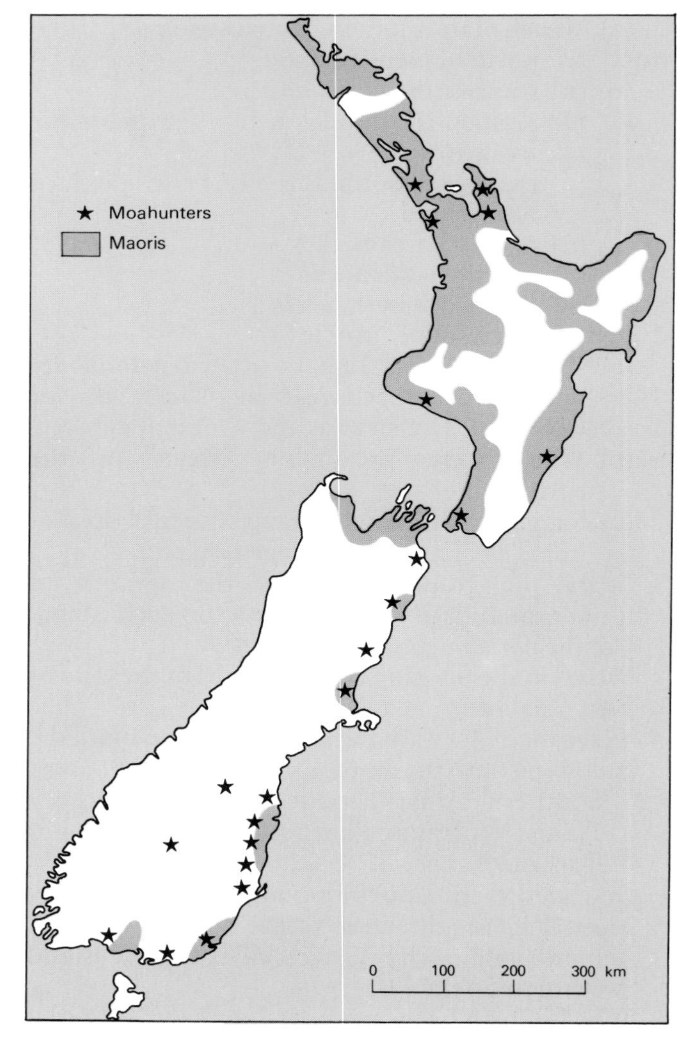

In 1769 James Cook, the English sea captain, made friendly contact with the Maoris on North Island. He went on to explore the east coast of Australia, and it was here the convict settlement of Sydney was set up in 1788. Ships sailed from Sydney to New Zealand.

The British Navy was the largest in the world. North Island provided timber for masts and flax for sails and rope. The Maoris cut the timber and prepared the flax and food. In return, they received clothes, blankets, axes, knives and guns.

The Maoris suffered from this contact with Europeans. Many died from diseases. Tribal warfare with guns cost more lives. Sugar and alcohol in their diet killed many more. But worse was yet to come because, as Maori numbers dwindled, more settlers arrived.

In 1840, Maori chiefs signed the Treaty of Waitangi, making Britain responsible for good order and development in the country. Organised settlement from Britain began. There were plenty of people in Britain seeking a better life. They came to planned settlements such as Wellington (1840) and Canterbury (1850). Graziers from Australia followed with merino sheep. They burned woodland on South Island to make pasture. There were 200 000 sheep in 1851 and 2 million in 1861. Feeding on the same pastures were rabbits and deer brought by the settlers.

Most settlers did not know how to farm in a highland area. When the trees were removed, the heavy rain washed away the soil and cut deep gullies into the slopes. This is called soil erosion.

The Maoris lost their land on North Island to the settlers. Skirmishes led to war and, by 1865, 2000 Maoris had been killed by British troops and the rest pushed into the interior. The number of Maoris had been cut from 250 000 to 42 000 in fifty years – the same fate as Australian Aboriginals (page 5). The settlers began to strip the forest from North Island. The best kauri trees were cut for timber (9) and the rest burnt down (10).

10 Forest clearance

9 Cutting kauri

Heavy rain often washed away the soil, but the settlers were not worried because there was plenty of land and they were making a good profit.

The first refrigerated ship reached Britain in 1882, with a cargo of frozen meat and butter. New Zealand had begun to supply Britain with food.

FOLLOW-UP WORK

1 Study map (8). Why did the Moahunters live mainly on South Island and the Maoris on North Island?
2 The Moahunters harmed the environment but the Maoris protected it. Why?
3 How did Europeans cause soil erosion?
4 Prepare notes for a discussion on the tribal lands of the Maoris. List reasons for
   (a) the Maoris keeping their tribal land,
   (b) the land being used by European settlers.

SOIL EROSION

The removal of soil by wind and rain at a faster rate than it is formed, particularly as a result of man's activities such as cutting down trees and overgrazing pasture. Gully erosion is the most dramatic form of erosion where rapidly flowing water cuts deep channels into hillsides.

SOIL EROSION: A WORLD PROBLEM

You can find out more about types of soil erosion and the worldwide scale of the problem. Ask for the worksheet.

Contrasts across South Island

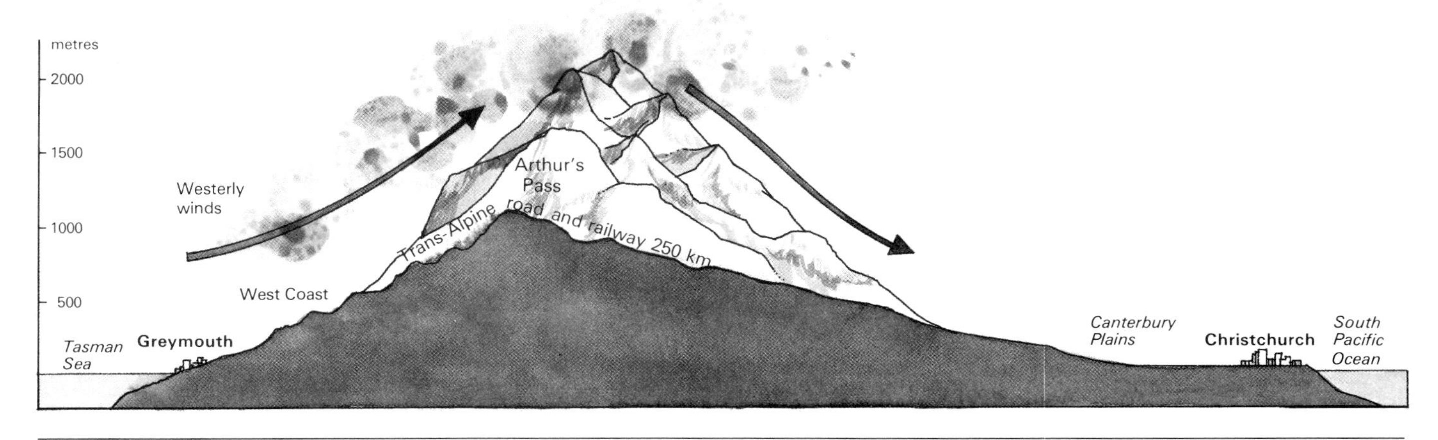

12 Across South Island

West Coast	*Contrasts*	*Canterbury Plains*
Rugged hills	The land	A gently sloping plain
Mainly granite	Rock	Deep gravel laid by rivers
Infertile clay soil. Poorly drained	Soil	Fertile loam soil. Well drained
Wet. Exposed to westerly winds. 3000 mm on the coast	Rainfall	Dry. In the rainshadow of the mountains. 650 mm on the coast
Winds off the sea. Summers warm, winters mild	Temperatures	Winds off the land. Summers hot, winters cold
Forest	Vegetation	Grassland
Gold and coal	Early European economy	Sheep and wheat
Declining. Coal, timber, livestock, fishing	Present economy	Expanding. Mixed farming, crops and livestock
Greymouth 7600 people Small commercial centre	Largest town	Christchurch 299 400 people Centre of industry, transport, trade and commerce

11 Southern Alps

The Southern Alps (11) rise to a height of 2100 metres. They form a barrier between the east and west sides of the island.

Study the differences between the land to the west of the mountains and the Canterbury Plains to the east (12).

FOLLOW-UP WORK

1 Why is the West Coast wetter than the Canterbury Plains?
2 Why are winters on the West Coast warmer than winters on the Canterbury Plains?
3 Why are the Canterbury Plains better farmlands than the West Coast?
4 Why is the West Coast a declining area and the Canterbury Plains an expanding one?

High country

Steep mountain slopes are New Zealand's high country. One-quarter of all the farmland is high country, but there are only 400 farms, called runs. The land is poor, and 10 000 hectares are needed to raise 10 000 merino sheep for their wool. Photograph (13) shows the sheep going out after dipping. They graze the tussock grassland on the higher slopes in summer. In winter, they must return to lower ground when snow blankets the mountains.

Life is hard and sheep losses heavy. There are no towns and no schools. The nearest neighbour is many kilometres away. Imagine that you are the runholder looking out over the yards (14). Farming has become difficult and you have asked the Lands and Survey Department to study your run. Their report has been made and you have to decide what to do. The problems are detailed below and numbered on the photograph (14).

1 Grass is not growing on the upper slopes. Loose rock (scree) covers steep slopes, and boulders from rockfalls are rolling onto good pastures.
2 Heavy rainfall has cut deep channels (gullies) into the hillslopes. A great deal of soil has been lost.
3 The mountain pastures have been burnt to help new grass to grow. Unfortunately this practice has damaged the soil.
4 There are deer and rabbits on the run. They could be eating as much grass as the sheep.

13 Sheep in the high country

5 There are too many sheep on the run. The price of wool is low so the size of the flock has been increased. There is not enough grass for their survival.
6 The best grazing blocks near the homestead are very poor quality compared with neighbouring runs.

Study the terms in the box before you tackle the problems on page 30.

14 Sheep in the yards

TERRACES

A series of wide steps cut into the hillside to retain the soil.

FODDER (forage) CROPS

Crops grown to feed to the animals.

ROTATION GRAZING

Controlled grazing of pasture where sheep are kept in one paddock for one day or more and then moved to another paddock to graze fresh grass.

WINDBREAK (shelterbelt)

A line of trees to break the force of the wind in an exposed area.

15 *Aerial spraying in high country*

Solving high country problems

On a recent visit to the government research station you have seen the advantages of spreading fertilizers over high country, from a light aircraft (15). The fertilizers provide nutrients which start a cycle of growth (16) which will help your pastures.

You have also asked the Soils and River Control Council to advise you on the best methods to solve your farming problems. They have made twelve suggestions which you must consider.

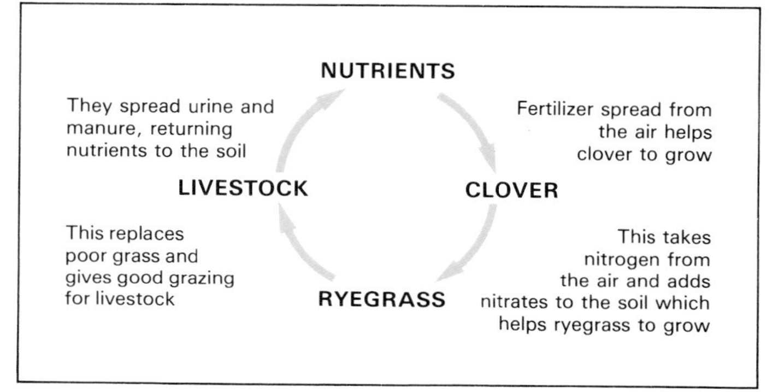

16 *Cycle of growth*

A Make terraces on the slopes near the homestead. This will prevent rock and soil movement on your best land.

B Sell half your sheep. Buy Aberdeen Angus and Hereford beef cattle. They will give a good profit and cause less damage to the pasture.

C Remove sheep from the upper slopes. Plough land near to the homestead and grow fodder crops for the sheep.

D Sow high-quality grass seed and clover from a light aircraft.

E Divide your best pasture into smaller paddocks and use rotation grazing.

F Build dams across all the gullies and fill with soil.

G Remove animal pests. Deer can be marketed as venison.

H Plant more trees as a windbreak. They will also prevent soil movement.

I Spread super-phosphate and lime fertilizer from a light aircraft.

J Stop burning the grassland. Buy spiked rollers and crush old grass. This will help new grass to grow.

K Dig channels to divert spring snow-melt into ponds. This will stop flood damage. The ponds will provide drinking water for the sheep in summer.

L Plant trees on high slopes. This will stop rock falls and control the amount of water washing over the surface.

FOLLOW-UP WORK

1 Which of the solutions listed **A** to **L** help to solve problems **2** and **6**?

2 Costs are high, so you will have to introduce the suggested improvements over a period of years. Make a rank order list of items **A** to **L**. Give reasons for the order you choose.

Farming on the Canterbury Plains

> *MIXED FARMING*
>
> Arable farming is the cultivation of the soil for crops. Pastoral farming is the rearing of animals. Mixed farming is the cultivation of crops *and* the rearing of animals.

17 Canterbury Plains

The Canterbury Plains are New Zealand's most productive farmlands. Sheltered from the prevailing westerlies by the Southern Alps (17), this is the driest part of the country and the best for growing crops and fattening lambs. The plains are a patchwork of fields for crops and animals. Sheep reared in the high country are brought here to produce lambs. Canterbury lamb is exported: one-third of all exports go to Britain. Wheat is the main crop of the plains. Barley, potatoes, vegetables and fruit are also grown to meet the needs of New Zealand's 3 million people. Fresh milk, eggs and poultry supply the daily needs of Christchurch.

This is mixed farming. Farmers produce more of what brings them the highest profit at the time, but keep a mixture of crops and animals for rotations.

Farms range in size from 80 to 200 hectares. The smallest farms are near Christchurch and produce food for the city. Further inland, on the wetter slopes and on stony soils, the land is best for pasture; more animals are kept and farms are large. Map (18) shows a farm near Christchurch. Wheat, peas and potatoes are cash crops. There is a flock of 350 ewes grazing five paddocks. There is one paddock of fodder for winter feed.

18 Plan of farm

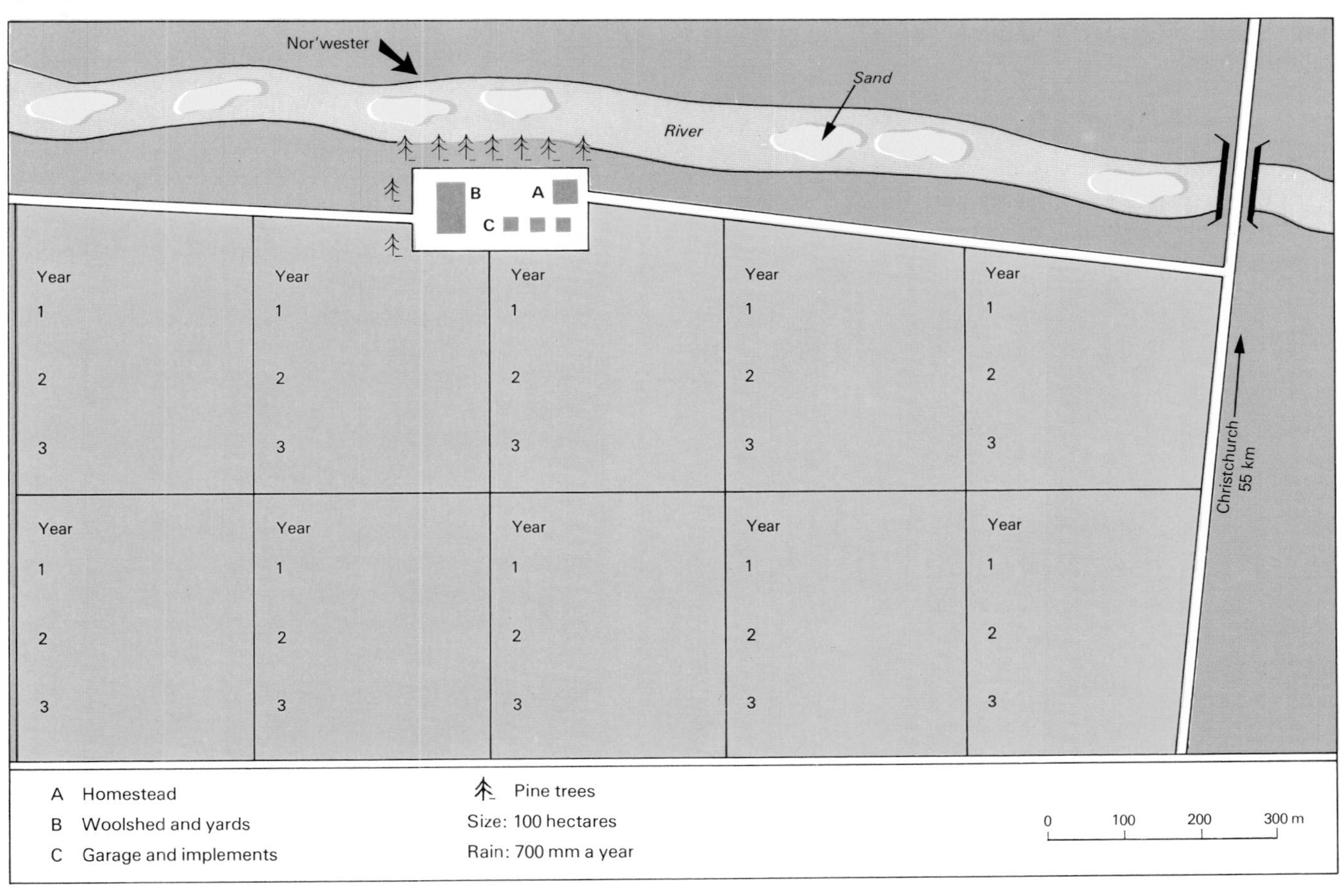

RUNNING A FARM

In a mixed farming area the farmer makes more decisions each year about what to produce than on any other type of farm. Imagine you are running the farm (18). Copy the farm plan. You will make decisions each year, for the next three years, and write your plans onto the map. This is a commercial farm and your aim is to make a profit. Your target is 85 points' combined profit from three years' farming.

Year 1 In the spaces for year 1, write the word SHEEP into five paddocks and FODDER into one paddock. You have to decide which cash crops to grow in the other four paddocks. Write the name of a crop – wheat, potatoes or peas – in each paddock. Ask for details of farming conditions and market prices. Work out your total profit for the year.

Year 2 You can decide to increase or reduce the size of the flock (work in blocks of seventy), grow one crop or a variety of crops. In the spaces provided for year 2, fill in the use for each paddock. Allow one paddock for fodder if you keep sheep, and think about the rotation of crops. Ask for conditions and prices and work out your profit for year 2.

Year 3 Complete the plan for year 3. Decide your profit for the year, the total profit over three years and decide whether you have made a success of farming.

> *COMMERCIAL FARMING*
>
> Producing food for sale rather than for the direct use of the grower. On the Canterbury Plains this includes cash crops such as wheat, vegetables and fruit.

19 Christchurch

FOLLOW-UP WORK

The farmer's decisions are affected by many physical, economic and human factors. As you answer each question, place its number into the correct box on your own copy of table (20).

1 The farmland is flat.
   (a) Why is flat land helpful to you?
   (b) Why is flat land difficult to drain?
   (c) How can you drain the heavier soils in the southern paddocks?
2 The farm is near the river.
   (a) Why is this helpful in summer?
   (b) What danger might there be in winter?
   (c) How have rivers made the plain fertile?
3 Soils in the northern paddocks are sandy.
   (a) Where does the sand come from?
   (b) Will this be a well-drained soil?
   (c) Will this favour pasture or vegetables?
4 Strong winds blow across the plains.
   (a) Which is the prevailing wind?
   (b) Why is this a dry wind?
   (c) How can the farmer protect the homestead and fields from the wind?
5 Your farm is small.
   (a) What might this tell you about the quality of the land?
   (b) How might the small size affect how you farm?
6 Your farm is near Christchurch (19).
   (a) How might this affect what you produce?
   (b) How will this affect the cost of transport of inputs and outputs?
7 Most farms are mixed farms.
   Did you continue mixed farming or specialise in years 2 or 3? Say why/why not.
8 Most farmers use crop rotation.
   Did you rotate your crops? Say why/why not.
9 Labour costs are high.
   The family is your only labour but most farmers hire extra labour for shearing and harvesting. Would you do this? Say why/why not.
10 Mixed farming is expensive.
   The cost of adding dairy cattle to your farm would be high but fresh milk is needed in Christchurch. What would you do? Say why.
11 Government subsidies and tax relief have been stopped. Prices of inputs and interest on loans are high but food prices have fallen. You will need to spend less on fertilizers and pesticides. Will this solve the problem? Say why/why not.

20 Factors affecting the farmer's decisions

Physical	*Economic*	*Human*

Dairy farming

New Zealand can make butter, send it halfway round the world to Britain, and sell it at a lower price than the cost of milk from Britain's own dairy farms. The map (21), photographs (22, 23) and facts about dairy farming (24) explain why this is possible.

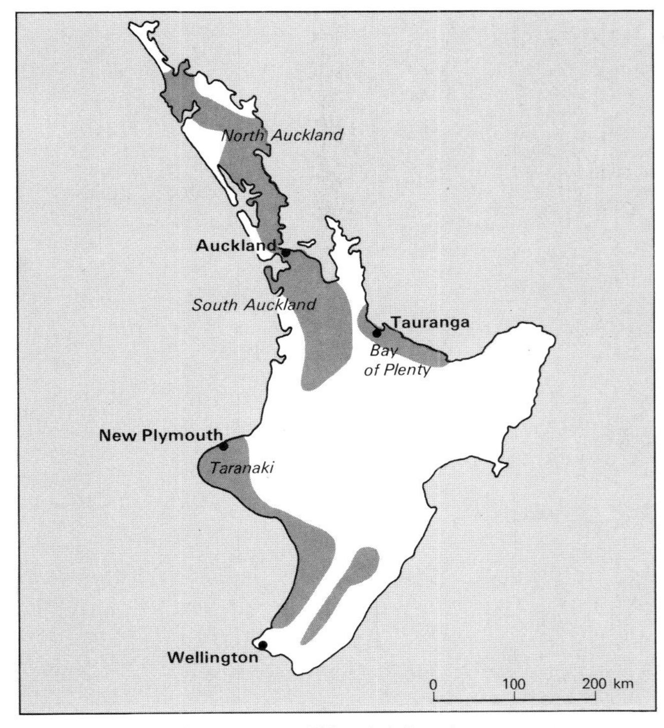

21 Dairy farming areas of North Island

FOLLOW-UP WORK

Use the list of factors (24) to do these exercises.

1 Name the *four* physical inputs and *three* human and economic inputs which favour dairy farming.

2 Name the *two* processes on the dairy farm which make this one of the world's most efficient farming systems.

22 Jersey cows, North Island

23 Making butter

3 Name the *three* factors concerned with the output of dairy farms which are of most importance in producing low-cost butter for Britain.

24 Factors favouring dairy farming

1 Warmth, sunshine and plentiful rainfall every month. These are ideal conditions for growing grass.
2 Mild winters. The grass grows in winter. Cattle graze out of doors all the year. This saves the cost of buildings and extra fodder crops.
3 Flat and gently sloping land. Large areas of North Island have suitable slopes for dairy cows (21, 22).
4 Fertile soils from volcanic ash. The soils are rich in nutrients for a good growth of grass.
5 Rotation grazing. Cattle graze the paddocks in rotation. This allows the grass to grow to its optimum height for grazing.
6 Breeding high-quality cattle. New Zealand Jersey cattle (22) give the most butterfat.
7 Specialised farming. Money is invested in the one farm activity, which reduces costs.
8 Low labour input. Labour costs are low because these are family farms.
9 Mechanised farms. Herringbone and rotary milking parlours milk large numbers of cattle as a continuous process which allows most farms to have 120 cows or more.
10 Guaranteed prices. The New Zealand Dairy Board pays a guaranteed price for butterfat which benefits the farmer when world prices are low.
11 Mechanised dairies. Butter is made in bulk at a low cost (23).
12 Cheap transport. The dairy regions are close to the coast where large refrigerated ships carry butter in bulk to Britain and other markets.
13 Market strategy. Selling large amounts to a few countries results in lower prices.

Depending on trade

New Zealand depends on trade, and the ports such as Lyttelton Harbour, Christchurch (25) are modern and busy. In the early years of colonisation the country sent food to Australia and wool to Britain. With the advent of the refrigerated ship, large amounts of meat and dairy products could be sent halfway round the world to London and arrive fresh and at a price people were willing to pay. Britain, in return, sent manufactured goods to New Zealand. Both countries benefited from this two-way trade. New Zealand concentrated upon producing large amounts of high-quality food at the lowest cost, knowing there was a secure market in Britain.

When Britain joined the European Economic Community (EEC) in 1973, all this changed. Taxes were placed on New Zealand products making them less competitive. A limit was set on the amount of food that could be sold in Britain and this amount was to be reduced each year. The effect on the sale of dairy products in Britain is shown in the graph (26).

New Zealand had to find new markets for milk, lamb and wool. Trying to sell dairy products was the most difficult of all. Many countries only trade within their own political circle of countries, and many others produce all the milk they need. Some do not eat dairy products, and others cannot afford to buy them. Added to these problems are the huge amounts of subsidised food that are being dumped onto the world market by the USA and EEC at low prices.

The newspaper article shows how complex the trade situation had become in 1988 (27).

25 Lyttelton Harbour

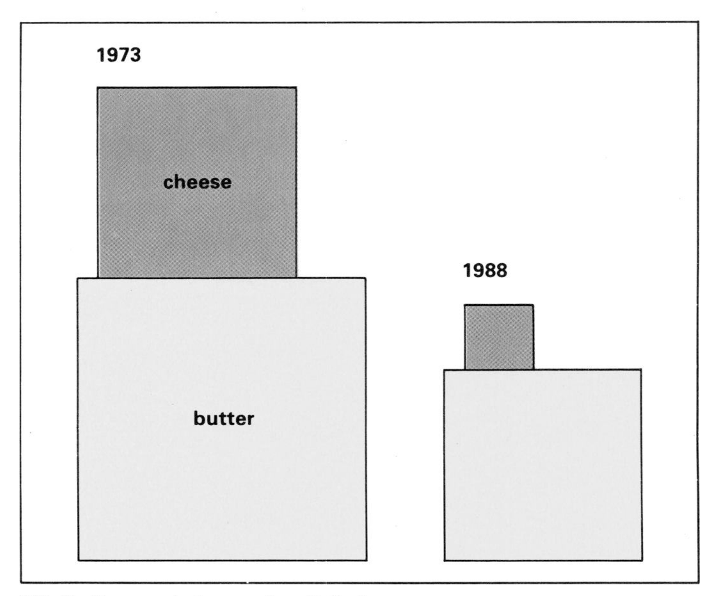

26 Butter and cheese for Britain

Changes in the composition and direction of trade are shown in the trade statistics tables (28), (29) and (30). Geographical ties in the Pacific world have been added to the historical ones with Britain.

FOLLOW-UP WORK

1 Copy map (21). A 10 000 tonne refrigerated ship is scheduled to bring 1000 tonnes of butter to Britain. The ship leaves Wellington (31), and calls at New Plymouth, Auckland and Tauranga, to load butter.
   (a) Mark the route of the ship on your map.
   (b) Mark an arrow from Tauranga in the direction the ship will travel to London.

27 News item adapted from Daily Telegraph *article, 10 May, 1988*

No point to butter ban

If New Zealand butter supplies to Britain were stopped by the Common Market, there would be no benefit to British and European dairy farmers, claimed the Chairman of the New Zealand Dairy Board in London yesterday. If the present quota of 74,500 tonnes of butter that New Zealand is allowed to send to Britain was reduced it would merely bring increased competition for EEC farmers in other markets of the world. "What we do not sell in the UK we must place somewhere else" said the Chairman.

Past cuts in the amount of dairy products sent here has simply meant New Zealand has made a better cheese to compete with the Danes on the Iranian market, or milk powder to compete with the Dutch in the Far East or the French in Algeria.

The Chairman said these butter sales to Britain were vital to New Zealand's economy and only represented a tiny 1.7 per cent of EEC milk production.

A survey in Britain found that 84 per cent of British consumers want New Zealand to be allowed to go on selling its butter here.

2 How did Britain joining the EEC affect sales of butter and cheese to Britain?
3 Study the newspaper article (27).
  (a) Why was the Chairman of the New Zealand Dairy Board in London?
  (b) What arguments are used to persuade the EEC not to cut New Zealand's quota of dairy product sales to the EEC?
  (c) Which four countries in the EEC which also produce dairy products are mentioned in the article?
  (d) Which three foreign markets, supplied by New Zealand and by the EEC with dairy products, are mentioned?
  (e) Why do EEC countries want New Zealand to sell less butter to Britain?
4 Why has New Zealand found it difficult to find new markets for dairy products?
5 Study tables (28) and (29).
  (a) What evidence is there in the statistics to suggest that New Zealand is becoming less dependent on farm products?

28 Types of exports (% by value)

Exports	*1965*	*1985*
Meat	29	20
Wool	28	14
Dairy products	27	12
Hides and skins	4	3
Timber and paper	2	5
Fruit and vegetables	1	3
Others: mainly manufactures	9	43

29 Types of imports (% by value)

Imports	*1965*	*1985*
Manufactured goods	71	64
Chemicals	10	12
Oil	8	14
Raw materials for industry	5	5
Food, drink and tobacco	6	5

31 Wellington Harbour

  (b) Draw pie graphs using the export statistics in table (28) to support your answer to (a).
  (c) Why is it better to have a variety of exports rather than one or two products?
6 Study table (30).
  (a) Draw pie graphs to show the markets for New Zealand's exports in 1890 and 1985. What major changes in the direction of trade do the graphs show?
  (b) 'New Zealand is now a country of the Pacific world rather than an outpost of Europe.' Do you agree?

STRUCTURE OF EMPLOYMENT

The jobs that people do are classified into the three economic sectors of the economy: primary, secondary and tertiary. The historical sequence in New Zealand is similar to that followed by many countries. Ask for the topic sheets which include exercises with a compound bar graph and a triangular graph.

30 Imports and exports (% by value)

	Britain		*Australia*		*USA*		*Japan*		*Other countries*	
	Exports to	*Imports from*	*Exports to*	*Imports from*	*Exports to*	*Imports from*	*Exports to*	*Imports from*	*Exports to*	*Imports from*
1870	52	58	46	36	–	1	–	–	2	5
1890	75	67	15	17	6	6	–	–	4	10
1910	84	62	9	14	3	8	–	–	4	16
1930	80	47	3	8	5	18	–	–	12	27
1950	66	60	3	12	10	7	–	–	21	21
1970	36	30	8	21	15	13	10	8	30	28
1975	22	19	11	20	12	13	12	14	43	34
1985	9	9	16	19	15	17	15	20	45	35

Industry

Forest products from North Island

The centre of North Island is a plateau made from lava that erupted from the interior of the Earth millions of years ago. On the surface of the lava is a layer of pumice rock which was formed from material thrown into the air during periods of volcanic activity.

At the end of the nineteenth century, settlers cleared the scrub and ferns from the plateau and sowed grass seed. The grass grew but the sheep and cattle became sick and died. The reason is now known to be the lack of the trace element cobalt in the pumice soils. Animals need cobalt, from the grass they eat, to remain healthy.

The government decided to plant pine trees over large areas of the plateau. This was done between 1923 and 1936 using unemployed men and prison labour. The trees thrived in the pumice soils and warm, damp climate. Within twenty-five to thirty years they were fully grown and ready for cutting. Paper mills were built at Kinleith in 1952 and Kawerau in 1955. Map (32) shows the location of the forests.

Photograph (33) shows part of the Kaingaroa Forest, which is one of the largest plantations in the world. When mature trees are felled, new seedlings are planted. This practice secures the forest industry for the future.

33 Kaingaroa Forest

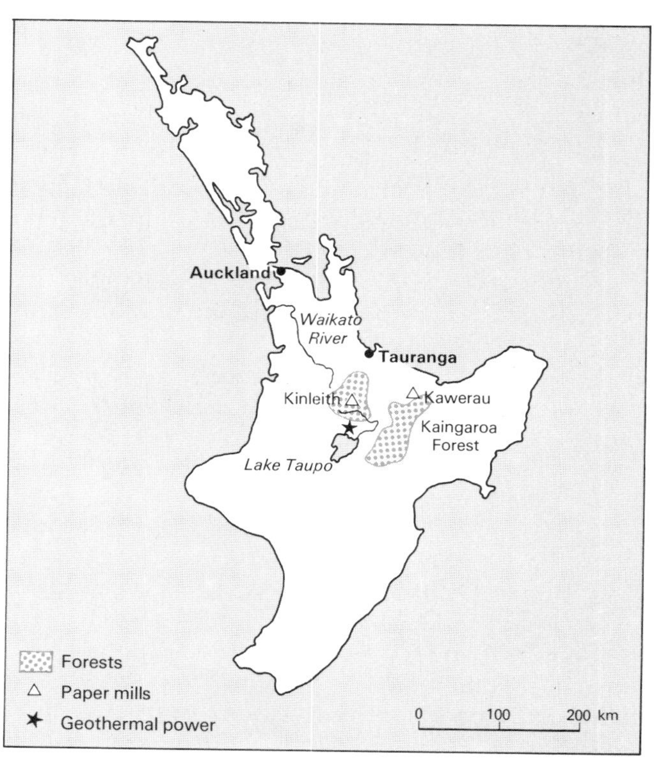

32 Forest industry of North Island

Advantages of forestry
- Provides jobs in rural areas
- Meets the country's timber needs and provides raw material for manufacturing industries
- Saves the cost of timber imports
- Provides export revenue making the economy less dependent on farm products. Japan and Australia are large markets
- Protects the soil from accelerated erosion
- Provides a habitat for wildlife

Problems of forestry
- Changes the natural forest and landscape into a manmade landscape of rows and blocks (33)
- Costs are high – twenty-five years must pass before the trees can be harvested
- A capital-intensive industry employing few people
- Clear-cut areas and large sawmills and paper mills spoil the environment and disturb wildlife
- The forest resource is benefiting Japan and Australia more than New Zealand
- Private forest limits public access

FOLLOW-UP WORK

1 Why is forest a renewable resource?
2 Why is Kinleith a good location for a paper mill?
3 Why is Tauranga a good location for a timber port?
4 Do the advantages of forestry outweigh the problems? Say why/why not.

North Island: power for industry

Pulp and paper mills need power. This comes from power stations in the Waikato Valley.

The Waikato River is the longest in New Zealand. It is shown on map (32). There are eleven power stations along the river between Lake Taupo and the sea. There are eight hydro-electric power (HEP) stations, using the power of rushing water to make electricity. The largest station is Maraetai (34).

There are two more power stations, south of Lake Taupo, using water diverted from lakes on the volcanic plateau. Study all these sites on the section (35).

Clouds of steam near the river at Wairakei (36) locate another source of power. The rocks in this area are hot, porous and contain water. A hundred boreholes have been drilled, some to a depth of 1200 metres. Water flows into the boreholes and boils. Steam is formed which rushes to the surface under great pressure. The steam is taken through pipes to the power station by the side of the river.

34 Maraetai power station

Water from the river is used for cooling at this power station and also at Huntly and Meremere. These two power stations make electricity from the Waikato Valley's third source of power.

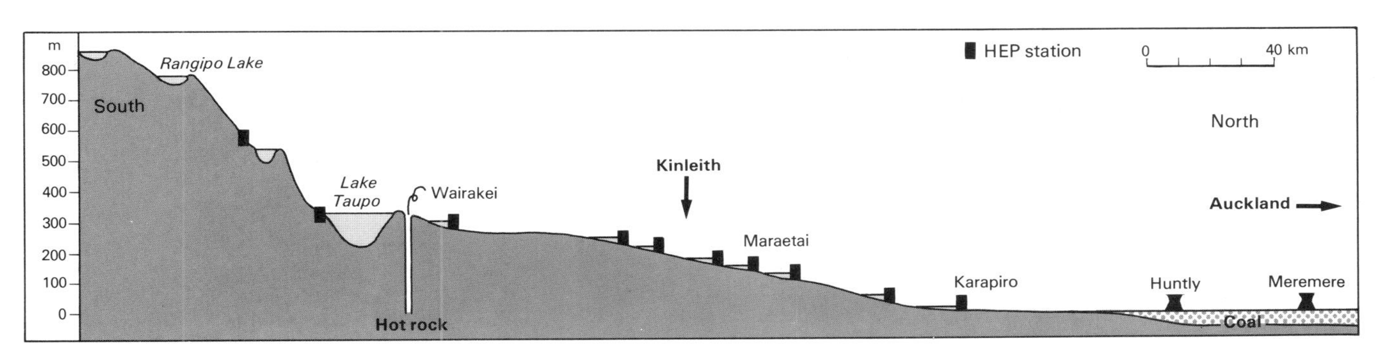

35 Longitudinal section of Waikato River

36 Geothermal steamfields

FOLLOW-UP WORK

1 Study the photograph (34).
   (a) Why was this a good site for building a dam?
   (b) How many power stations are there at this site?
   (c) The dam has formed Lake Maraetai, which covers three square kilometres of land. How can the lake be used?
2 Study photograph (36). Why is the power station not on the steamfields, which are shown here?
3 Study section (35).
   (a) Why are there no hydro-electric power stations below Karapiro?
   (b) How many times is the water from Rangipo Lake used to make hydro-electricity before it reaches the sea?
   (c) Why are there hot rocks in this area?
   (d) How is electricity made at Huntly?
   (e) Name two uses for electricity shown on the section.

Aluminium from South Island

The largest hydro-electric power station in New Zealand is at Lake Manapouri, shown on map (37) and photograph (40). Electricity made here is used at the aluminium smelter at Bluff (38), on the southern tip of South Island.

The raw material comes from Australia (page 6). Bauxite (aluminium hydroxide) mined at Weipa, in northern Queensland, is sent by bulk-carrier ship to Gladstone, shown on map (39). It is refined at Gladstone into a white powder called alumina (aluminium oxide). A great deal of electricity is needed to break the bond between the aluminium and the oxygen in the alumina. The electricity is available at Lake Manapouri. The alumina is shipped to Bluff where the aluminium is made. Four tonnes of bauxite at Weipa are used to make two tonnes of alumina at Gladstone which give one tonne of aluminium at Bluff.

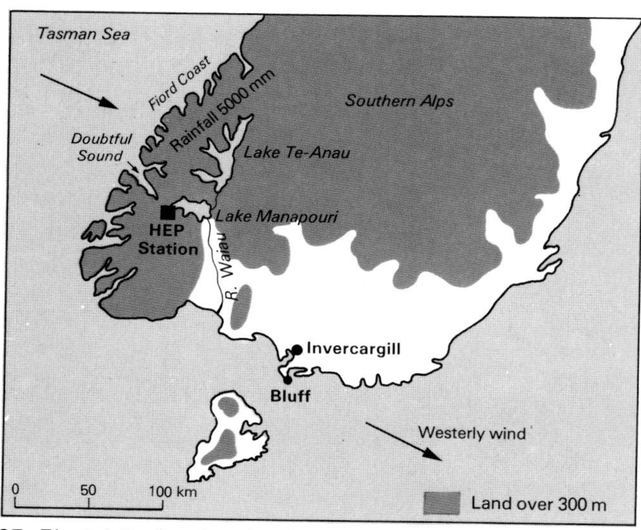

37 *Electricity for the aluminium industry*

38 *Aluminium smelter at Bluff*

The smelter at Bluff is half-owned by Japanese companies and half the aluminium is sent to Japan. This is one example of the links which are made between countries in the Pacific world.

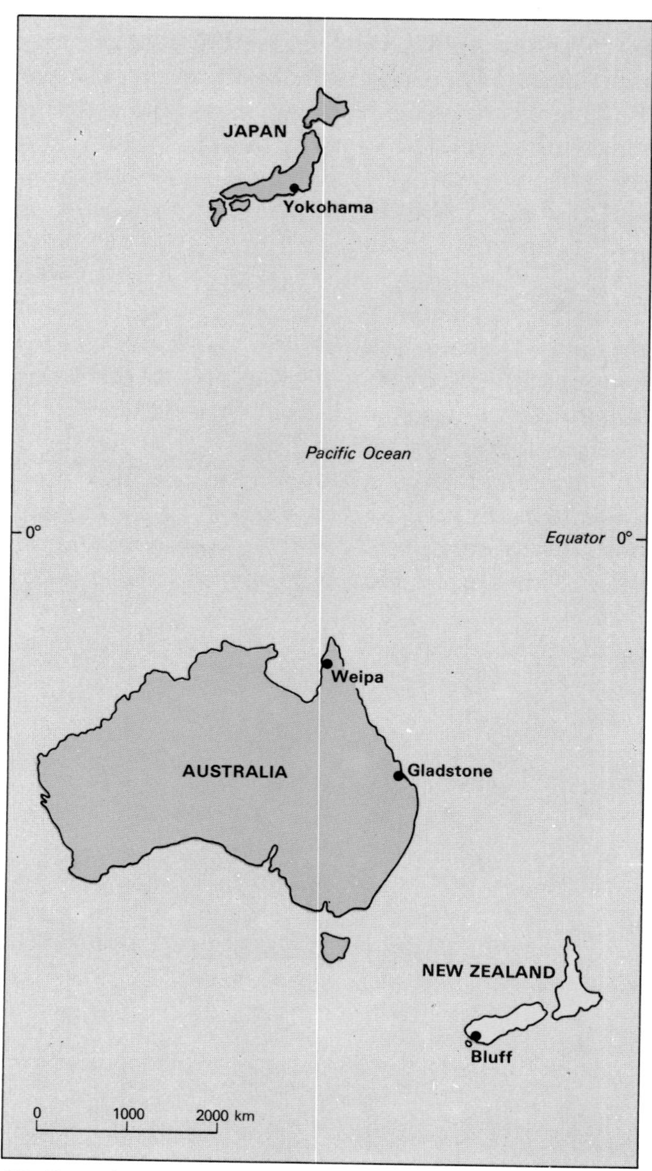

39 *From bauxite to aluminium*

FOLLOW-UP WORK

1 Study map (37) and photograph (40). Why is this a very favourable area for hydro-electric power?
2 Study photograph (38) and map (37). What advantages are there for siting the aluminium smelter at Bluff?
3 Copy map (39). Mark coloured arrows to show transport routes for bauxite, alumina and aluminium.

THE MANAPOURI DEBATE

In 1960, the New Zealand government asked the Australian aluminium company Comalco to build a smelter at Bluff. The government would build a power station at Lake Manapouri (40) to supply electricity to the smelter. Comalco would have full rights to the waters of Lake Manapouri, Lake Te-Anau and the Rivers Waiau and Mararoa (41). The government wanted the scheme because it would bring industry to New Zealand, jobs to South Island and a supply of aluminium for other industries. Comalco would benefit from a free supply of electricity.

The project went ahead. The government built the power station and the company built the smelter. The first aluminium was produced in 1971.

During the building of the power station and the smelter, the government signed a new agreement with the company. The plan was to raise the level of Lake Manapouri by eight metres. This would be done by building a dam across the River Waiau, which is the natural outlet for the lake. Raising the lake would link it to Lake Te-Anau and greatly increase the amount of water that could be stored. The power station could make more electricity and the smelter could then make more aluminium.

Many people said the lake must not be made bigger because it would drown many islands, destroy forest and wildlife, cover the beaches and change the appearance of the area. Also, the lake is in Fiordland National Park which is a protected area.

The greatest debate in the history of New Zealand took place and a Government Commission was set up to inquire into the new scheme.

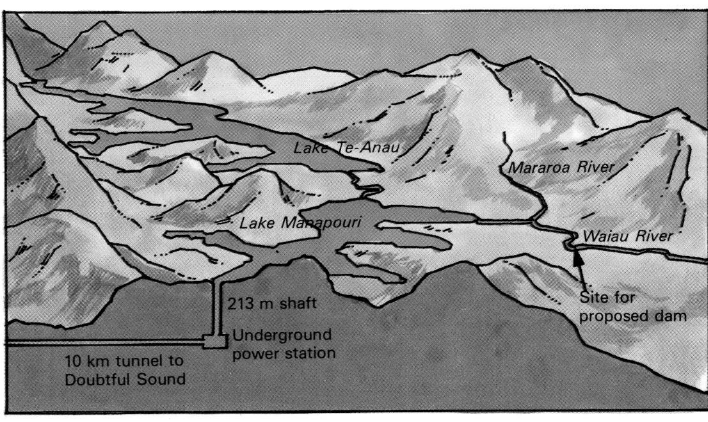

41 Sketch of lake area

The issues

Do we want to risk the beauty of our national park for the sake of electric power? The government is committed to supply power to the Comalco smelter and this industry will earn New Zealand $25 million a year, but is the price too great to pay?

The final decision will be a landmark in the history of New Zealand's development.

The debate

Four speakers are required: two speak on behalf of the company and two represent the Nature Conservation Council. The speakers for the company must prepare arguments in favour of the new scheme. The conservation group must prepare arguments against the scheme. Each speaker has a few minutes to put his case to the class and each seconder can add extra points, following a class discussion.

A vote is taken at the end of the debate to decide whether the lake level should be raised or left at its natural height.

Ask for the real outcome of the debate.

40 Lake Manapouri

Cities

Although New Zealand owes its prosperity to the products of the countryside, mechanised pastoral farming is labour-efficient and only 10 per cent of the labour force work on farms. Most people live in cities where they work in factories, offices, shops, restaurants, hotels and in a wide range of community and personal services. The statistics in table (42) show the growth of towns and cities this century.

Urban life has always been a feature of European settlement in New Zealand. The first settlers came from towns in Britain. Dunedin grew rapidly when gold was discovered there in 1861. Christchurch prospered when the refrigerated ship came into use in 1882. Wellington (43) expanded when it was chosen as capital city in 1865. Auckland was the main settlement in the north. These four towns were service centres for agricultural hinterlands and ports for trade with Britain. They grew even more when farming became mechanised, mining declined, transport centred there, factories were built and services established. The statistics in table (44) shows the importance of the four cities.

42 Urban and rural population proportions

Year	% urban	% rural
1906	48	52
1916	54	46
1926	67	33
1936	67	33
1946	71	29
1956	74	26
1966	79	21
1976	83	17
1986	84	16

43 Wellington

FOLLOW-UP WORK

1 Study table (42). Draw a line graph to show how the proportion of New Zealand's urban population changed between 1906 and 1986. Use a scale of 4% per centimetre on the vertical axis, which should start at 48%.

2 Study table (44).
   (a) What changes occurred in the size and importance of the four cities between 1896 and 1986?
   (b) Describe the spacing of the four cities. Suggest a reason for this.
   (c) What advantage is there in the position of Wellington as capital city?

3 Study photograph (43) of Wellington. How has the hilly land affected buildings
   (a) at the centre of the city,
   (b) on the outskirts?

44 Main cities

% of NZ population	Population 1896	City	Population 1986	% of NZ population
8	57 600	Auckland	821 000	25
5	41 800	Wellington	326 000	10
7	51 300	Christchurch	300 000	9
6	47 300	Dunedin	107 000	3

Auckland: the drift to the north

In the early years of European settlement, most people lived on South Island. There were good pastures, gold and freedom from Maori wars. By 1901, the Maoris were defeated and dairy farming was growing on North Island. Since that time more people have moved northwards (45) and particularly to the city of Auckland (46).

45 North and South Island population proportions

Year	% of population N. Island	S. Island
1901	53	47
1921	62	38
1951	68	32
1971	72	28
1986	74	26

The main reasons people moved north are these:

- Warmer climate than the south
- More favourable land for farming
- New industries based on forests and natural gas
- Jobs in Wellington, the capital, in administration and business
- Attractions of Auckland (46, 47, 48); New Zealand industries are often one big factory and Auckland is the biggest market and best location. A snowball effect: as more people arrive more jobs in services are created.

49 Auckland

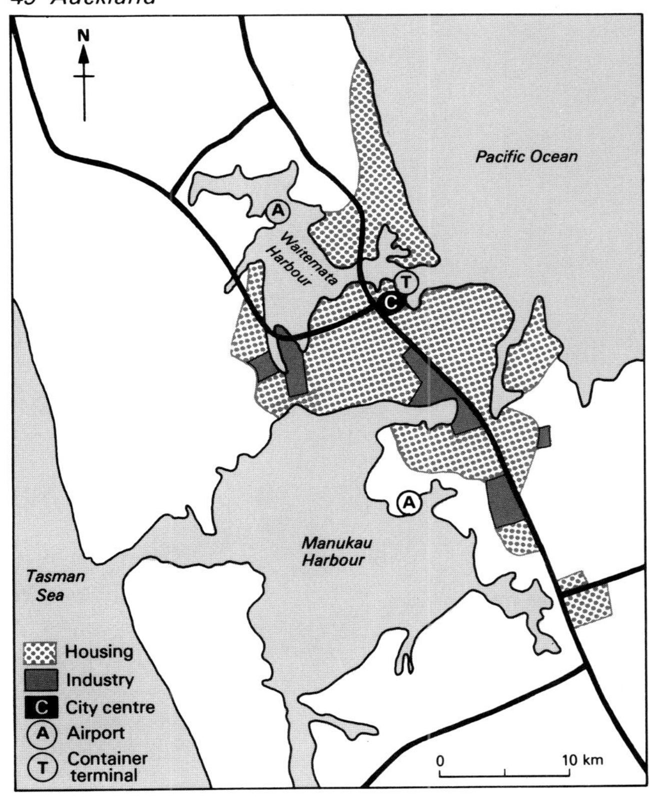

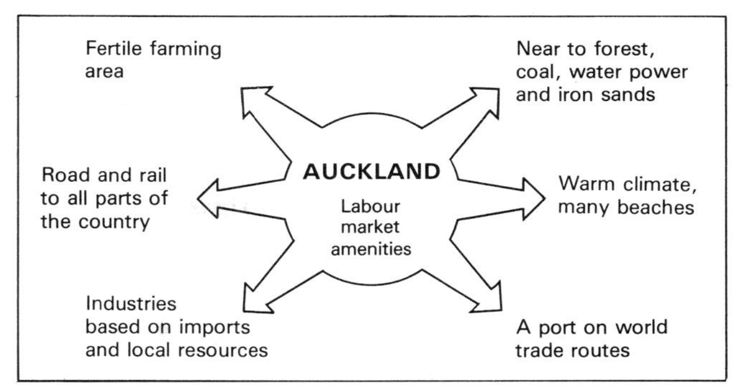

46 Reasons for the growth of Auckland

47 Auckland city centre

48 Auckland suburbs

FOLLOW-UP WORK

1. Draw pie graphs for 1901 and 1986 using the statistics in table (45). Describe the changes shown there.
2. Why would a company find Auckland a good location for a factory?
3. What problems might be created as a result of further drift of population to Auckland (a) for Auckland, (b) for South Island?

INTERNAL MIGRATION

The movement of people within the boundaries of a country including movement from rural to urban areas and a drift from less-favoured to favoured parts of the country.

Japan

1 *Mountains and crowded valleys*

Land of hazards

Japan consists of four large islands and more than three thousand small ones. Mountains form 72 per cent of the land, which means that 123 million people (1988) are crowded together on small areas of flat land, as shown in photograph (1). Factories, farms and houses are all cramped for space at the foot of the forested mountain slopes.

The Japanese are threatened by hazards that could strike from either the land or the sea. Japan lies at the place where plates of the Earth's crust are straining against each other, causing earthquakes. (Refer to page 24.) When the Earth trembles most people think of the Great Kanto Earthquake. On 1st September 1923, when people in Tokyo were cooking on open-fire stoves, an earthquake lifted and shook the ground. Fires swept through the wooden buildings of the city and 143 000 people were killed. This earthquake, which destroyed Tokyo, also caused a huge sea wave, called a tsunami, which swept inland at a height of ten metres, destroying all before it. Most cities feel the effects of 100 earthquakes each year. Read the

2 *From* The Times, *13th June 1978*

Violent earthquake strikes central Japan

From Peter Hazelhurst
Tokyo, June 12

A severe earthquake today jolted the north-eastern coast of Japan's central island, Honshu. It caused a series of landslips, disrupting electricity and water supplies in big towns and halting rush-hour commuter trains in Tokyo.

The police reported tonight that at least 21 people had been killed and 350 injured by falling buildings or debris.

The rolling earthquake, with its epicentre 60 miles off the eastern coast, struck the island at 5.15 JST this afternoon.

Seismologists said tonight that it registered 7.5 on the Richter scale at its epicentre.

Radio and television broadcasts warned the heavily populated coastal towns that a two-metre tidal wave would strike the Honshu coast tonight. But later the warnings were withdrawn.

Most of the casualties were reported 180 miles north-east of Tokyo in Miyagi prefecture where the earthquake went on for a whole minute. Streets in Sendai city were ruptured, water mains burst and electricity supplies were cut off.

Although no bad casualties were reported in the crowded urban areas of Tokyo and Yokohama, thousands of hysterical office workers rushed out of high-rise city buildings and on to the streets.

The rolling tremor, one of the worst in Japan since the war, came as an unpleasant shock to the capital. Only last week city dwellers were warned in an official municipal report that at least 36,000 persons were expected to die if Tokyo was hit by an earthquake as strong as that which struck and almost destroyed the capital in 1923.

The great Kanto disaster then claimed the lives of an estimated 143,000 victims. Tokyoites have since lived uneasily on top of one of the world's most unstable geological formations.

This afternoon women screamed and office workers clung to passage walls as tall buildings in the capital creaked and swayed to and fro at alarming angles for almost a minute. Water pipes burst and glass from windows crashed on to the pavement in front of at least one city building. Flights at Haneda airport were suspended for several hours while a damaged radar tower was repaired.

(The Uppsala seismological Institute in Sweden said the earthquake was the most powerful recorded anywhere in the world this year, Reuter reports.)

3 *Collapsed building at Sendai*

newspaper account (2) of the Sendai earthquake in 1978. One of the collapsed buildings is shown in photograph (3).

Earthquakes are when the ground shakes because plates are moving against each other or cracks occur in a subducting plate. Japan lies on the eastern edge of the Eurasian plate where both the Pacific plate and Philippine plate push beneath it (4). The point where the earthquake occurs is called the origin or focus. Shock waves radiate outwards from this point and are felt first, and with greatest force, directly above the focus, at a point called the epicentre (5). The intensity of the shock waves at the surface gets less as they move away from the epicentre. Observers at 118 earthquake observation stations spread across the country use the scale in table (6) to estimate the intensity of the earthquake at the station. High-performance seismometers are used to find the position and depth of the origin and register the energy of the original shock on the logarithmic Richter scale, from 0 to 9. The Great Kanto Earthquake registered 7.9.

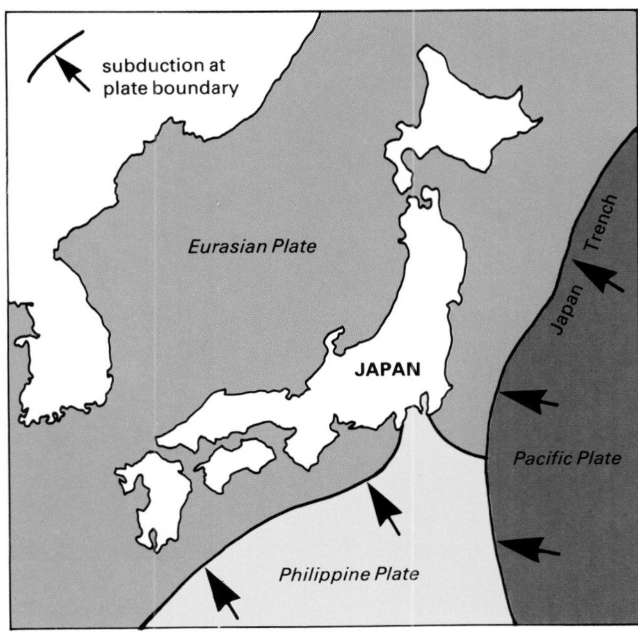

4 Japan: where three plates meet

5 Earthquake in Japan

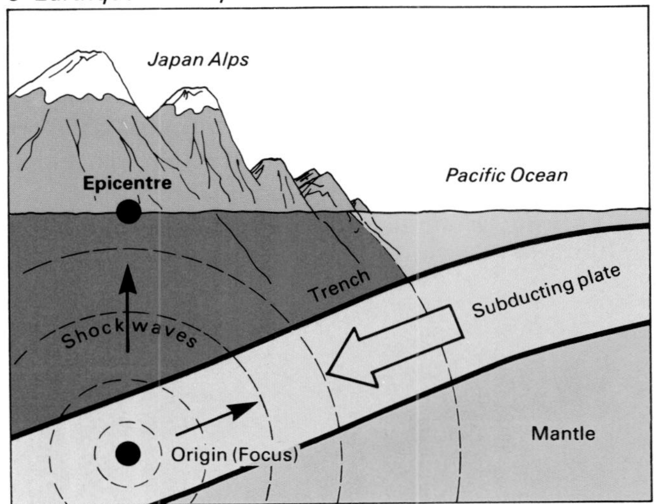

6 The Japanese earthquake scale

Rating number	*Description*	*Effects*
0	No feeling	Shocks too weak to be felt by humans, registered only by a seismograph
1	Slight	Extremely feeble shocks only felt by persons at rest or by those who are sensitive to an earthquake
2	Weak	Shocks felt by most persons, slight shaking of doors and Japanese latticed sliding doors (*shoji*)
3	Rather strong	Slight shaking of houses and buildings, rattling of doors and Japanese latticed sliding doors (*shoji*), swinging of hanging objects like electric lamps, moving of liquids in vessels
4	Strong	Strong shaking of houses and buildings, overturning of unstable objects, spilling of liquids out of vessels.
5	Very strong	Cracks in the walls, overturning of gravestones, stone lanterns, etc., damage to chimneys and mud-and-plaster warehouses
6	Disastrous	Demolition of houses, some landslips, fissures in the road and the ground
7	Very disastrous	Demolition of houses, intense landslips, large fissures in the ground and faults

Tsunami forecasts are given within 20 minutes of an earthquake and are made known to the public on the radio and television. Seventeen of Japan's seventy active volcanoes are kept under constant watch in order to warn the public of an eruption. Early warnings give people time to evacuate the danger area and so help to avoid a disaster.

FOLLOW-UP WORK

1 Study maps (4) and (7). Which plates caused
   (a) the Kanto earthquake,
   (b) the Sendai earthquake?
2 Why are millions of Japanese worried when an earthquake epicentre is located
   (a) in the Pacific Ocean,
   (b) near the south coast?
3 What factors caused the Kanto earthquake to be one of the world's worst disasters?

Japan lies across the path of monsoon winds, as shown in map (7). North-west monsoon winds bring heavy snow to the north and west of Japan in winter. In spring, the snow melts and water rushes down the mountains and floods the lowland. In summer, the south-east monsoon brings heavy rain to the south and east coasts. During this season, typhoons strike. Study the typhoons on the photograph of the Pacific world on page 1.

A typhoon is an intense tropical storm with winds reaching 160 km.p.h. Torrential rain brings floods and landslides. On 2nd September 1974, Typhoon Polly hit Tokyo. Photograph (8) shows the surging waters of the River Tama carrying away a house from the outskirts of the city. Seven thousand people evacuated their homes.

In 1959, the Ise Bay Typhoon hit Nagoya killing 5000 people and destroying 150 000 buildings. Photograph (9) was taken at the height of the storm. The floodwaters took two years to drain away.

7 Hazards in Japan

8 Floods following Typhoon Polly

9 Typhoon hits Nagoya

DISASTER PREVENTION

Cities are crowded into the narrow lowlands between the mountains and the sea. The city, shown in (10), has spread over the lower slopes of the mountains. Sand and city refuse have been used to reclaim land from the sea. Oil storage tanks, timber yards and houses have been built on the reclaimed land. Earthquakes and typhoons threaten the city.

Working in small groups, study the report on page 45, which outlines the dangers the city has to face.

Discuss each part of the report. Suggest ways of preventing or reducing the effects of the dangers listed there. Include early warning systems, emergency instructions for the people, and practical ways of preventing disasters, including major rebuilding projects.

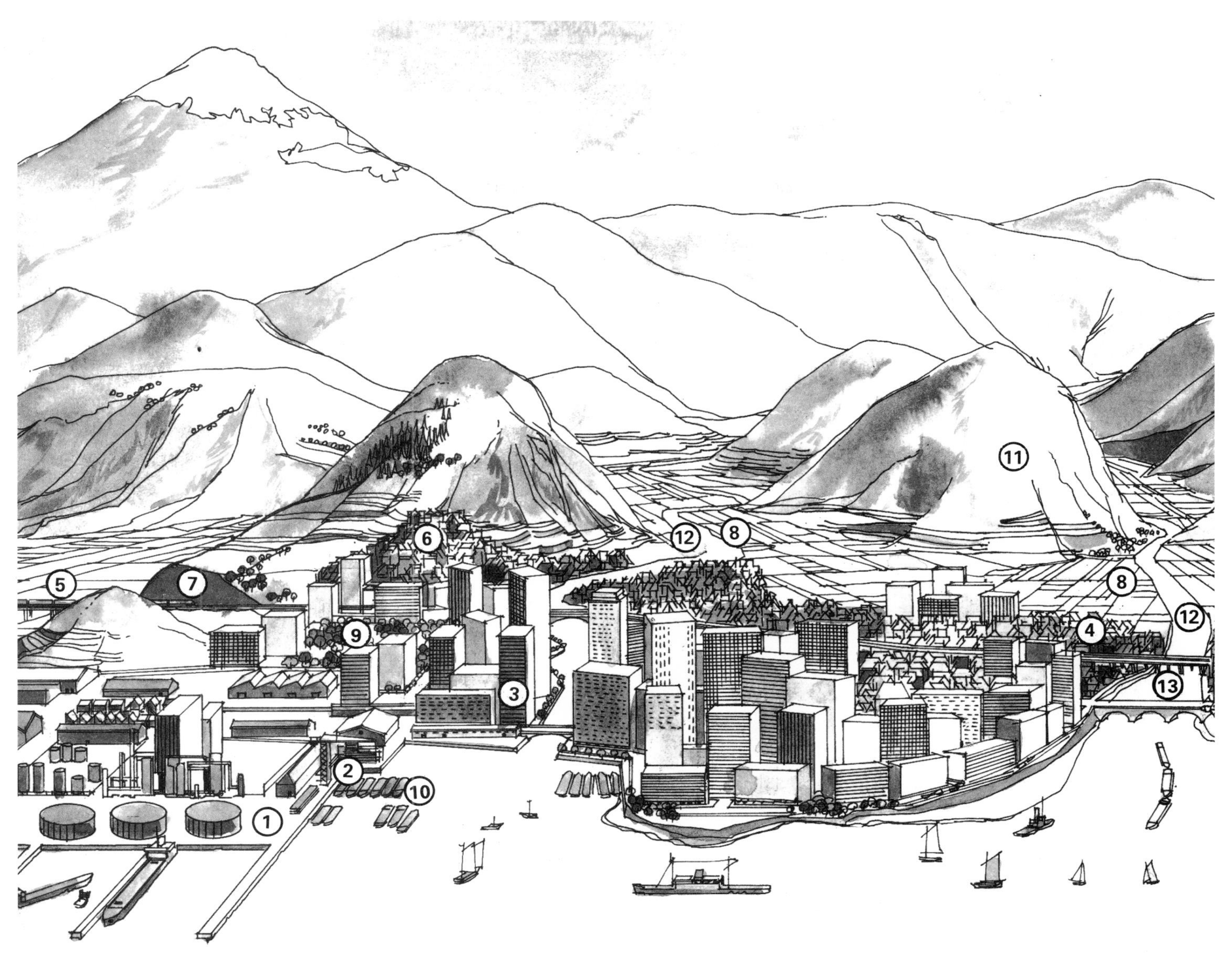

10 Sketch of a city

Earthquakes

1 Shock waves from an earthquake will be strongest on the reclaimed land which is not stable. The oil storage tanks ① may be damaged and fires spread to the timber yards ②. Housing on this land will be destroyed with possible loss of life.

2 Tall buildings in the city centre ③ may collapse. If an earthquake occurs during the working day, there will be great loss of life.

3 Wooden houses in the eastern part of the city ④ have open fires. If an earthquake occurs during the evening, fires will sweep through the houses and cause a huge loss of life.

4 The old viaduct ⑤ will collapse during a severe earthquake. This will remove the only land route to the west.

5 Landslides which follow an earthquake could damage the new housing on the foothills ⑥. The road and railway in the cutting ⑦ will be blocked. There will be some loss of farmland ⑧.

Typhoons

6 Violent winds will destroy some of the old wooden houses and blow down trees in the park ⑨. There will be damage to vessels ⑩ and tall cranes at the harbour.

7 With the passing of the typhoon, heavy rain will gully the slopes ⑪ and choke the rivers with silt ⑫.

8 Rivers will flood, destroying bridges ⑬ and houses on the flood plain.

9 Landslides will follow heavy rain and this could damage the housing on the foothills ⑥, block the cutting ⑦ and cover farmland ⑧.

Farming: a changing way of life

Mountains limit the amount of farmland to only 14 per cent of the whole country. This means that Japan's 4 million farms are very small. Most farmers have one hectare to feed their families and have a little food to sell.

Rice is the main crop. In the south of Japan, farmers grow rice in summer, and wheat, barley and vegetables in the mild winter months. Farms are too small to raise beef cattle so most people eat fish, pigs and poultry. Tea is the main drink and this crop is grown on the hillsides in southern Japan. There is so little flat land in Japan that farmers have made terraces on the sides of hills and mountains (11). Many changes occur in the use of the land from the flat land of the valley to the top of the hills. Study these changes on the sketch (12).

11 Terraced slopes near Tokyo

12 Changes in farming with height

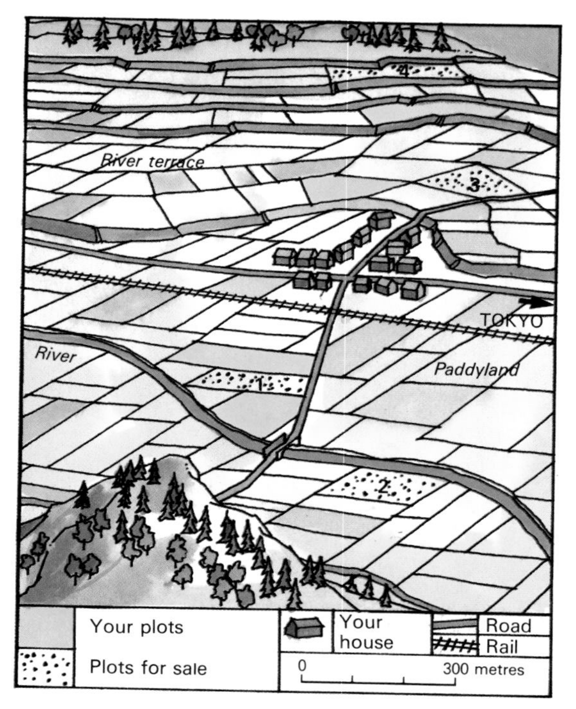

13 Farmland near Tokyo

A farm near Tokyo

This is a family farm with two hectares of land divided into four plots, which are scattered across the valley thirty kilometres from Tokyo (13). Study the area on the sketch.

The family includes two grandparents, father, who is head of the house, his wife, two sons aged 18 and 20 and a daughter aged 16. They live in a hamlet sited along the edge of the paddyland.

The two lowland plots are flooded in summer and planted with rice. Rice is eaten at every meal, and the family grows enough for its own needs with a little surplus for sale. The only modern machinery on the farm is a power cultivator which is used to prepare the land for planting (14). The rice seed is sown in the nursery beds near the house in April and the seedlings are transplanted into the two valley plots in May. These are busy times for the family because all the work is done by hand. The ground is weeded and hoed regularly during the summer before harvesting, by sickle, takes place in October. A winter crop of wheat is planted when the fields are cleared of rice.

The small plot of land on the river terrace is cultivated for wheat, barley, cabbages, radishes, peas and beans. The plot on the hillside terrace is planted with mulberry bushes. The leaves of the mulberry bush are fed to silkworms that are reared in the house during the summer. The family keep one dairy cow and twenty chickens. They collect wood and humus from the forest.

14 *Power cultivator in paddyfield*

All the products for sale from the farm are marketed through the local farmers' co-operative.

Owing to the small amount of farmland in Japan, the plots are intensively cultivated.

FOLLOW-UP WORK

1 Imagine that you are helping to make decisions for the farming family.
   (a) A family has left the hamlet and four plots of land are for sale (13). You can afford one of these. Which plot will you choose?
   (b) Many farmers are replacing mulberry bushes with fruit, vegetables and rice seedlings under plastic. What are your plans for the terrace plot?
   (c) A Tokyo company is marketing a rice transplanting machine at a low price (15). Do you want to buy a machine or continue with your hand methods?

15 *Rice transplanting by machine*

   (d) There is a demand for meat and dairy products in Tokyo. Should you rear pigs, poultry and dairy cows?
   (e) The farmers want to spray all the cropland with insecticide in June. Will you join with the others, spray at your own convenience or not spray at all?

INTENSIVE CULTIVATION

Applying either a large amount of capital or labour, or both of these, to a small plot of land in order to obtain a high yield of crops per hectare. This system of farming includes a high input of fertilizer, possibly irrigation and the production of several crops in one year.

   (f) Your main source of fertilizer is human excrement, and humus from the forest. Should you buy any chemical fertilizer?
   (g) Should any members of the family look for work in the offices and factories of Tokyo?

2 (a) Study the climate figures in table (16) and decide whether A or B applies to your farm. Give reasons for your decision.

16 *Climate figures for two farms*

	Month	*Jan*	*Apr*	*July*	*Oct*
A	Temp. (°C)	4	14	25	17
	Rain (mm)	49	122	140	203
B	Temp. (°C)	−5	6	21	11
	Rain (mm)	124	65	94	105

   (b) How do the climatic conditions, shown for your farm, favour the cultivation of rice?

3 In what ways is farming affected by (a) having a small farm, (b) being near to Tokyo?

17 *Changes in population and farming, 1955–85*

	1955	*1985*
Population of Japan (millions)	90	121
Population living on farms (millions)	37	20
Number of farms (millions)	6	4
% of farm income from non-farming activities	35	75
Average rice yield (tonnes per hectare)	3	4
Japan's self-sufficiency in food (% of food consumed)	92	70

4 Study statistics (17) and explain the following:
   (a) The size of farms is increasing.
   (b) Farms remain very small.
   (c) Land consolidation, which means allocating land to farmers in one block, replacing scattered plots, helps farmers.
   (d) Rice yields have risen since 1955.
   (e) Japan is less self-sufficient in food than in the past.
   (f) Most farms are run by elderly people and women.
   (g) Most arable farms are near cities and produce food for them.
   (h) The government subsidises rice farming.
   (i) Japan can buy rice from the USA, but chooses not to do so.

The growth of industry

A little over a hundred years ago, most of the 30 million Japanese were subsistence farmers. Since that time Japan has become an advanced industrialised country. Industrial growth brought increased prosperity which caused a rapid rise in population because people could afford to feed larger families.

The southern, warmer parts of the country most favoured for farming were also ideal locations for industry and this is where most of Japan's 120 million people live now.

A model of economic growth shows that countries often pass through five stages. These are shown for Japan in table (18). The structure of employment changed (19) as Japan became an industrialised country.

Big companies with large factories have been at the heart of Japan's industrial growth. This is shown on the network (20). Mitsubishi is one of these companies. Mitsubishi began in 1857 with an ironworks in Nagasaki and grew by building a shipyard in 1870. By the 1980s the company had expanded its operations, employing 64 000 people in twelve factories located in the main industrial belt of Japan (21). This is an integrated operation with close co-operation between the factories. Study sketch (22) which shows all the products that are made in Mitsubishi factories. This is a multinational company with branch operations in many countries, particularly in Europe and North America.

19 Structure of employment, 1880–1988

Year	*% primary*	*% secondary*	*% tertiary*
1880	82	6	12
1930	50	20	30
1950	48	22	30
1960	33	29	38
1970	20	33	47
1980	10	35	55
1988	8	34	58

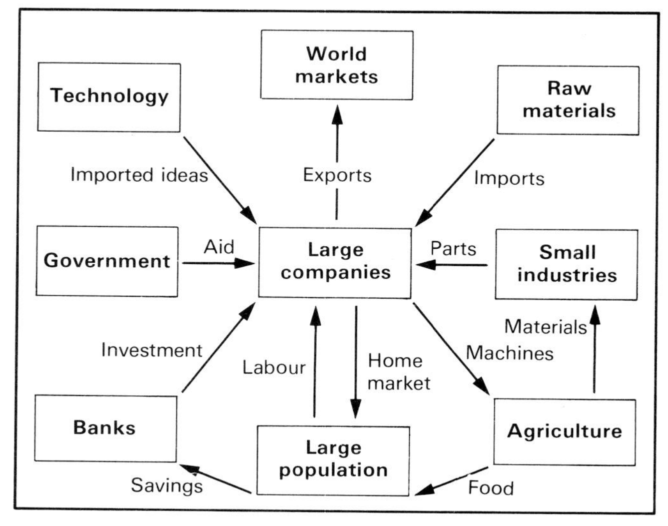

20 Network of factors for industrial growth

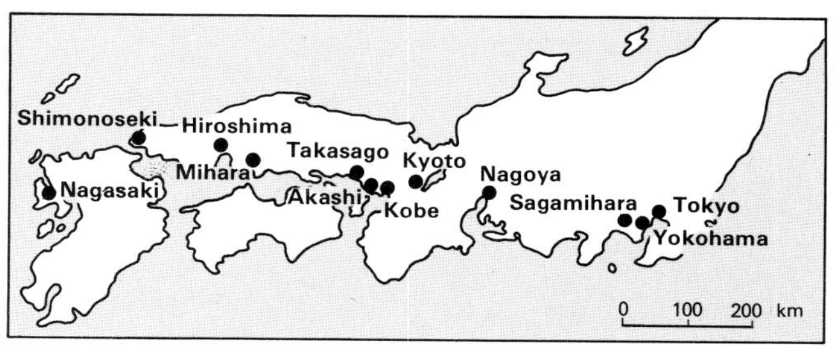

21 Mitsubishi factories

18 Stages in Japan's economic growth

Stage of economic growth	*Years*	*Details*
1	Before 1868	Subsistence farming with craft industries such as silk cloth, paper and ceramics.
2	1868 to 1880	A new strong government made improvements in farming to raise taxes and surplus food for industrial growth. Coal and copper mines opened. Roads improved and railways built.
3	1880 to 1930	Rapid industrial growth with big factories making textiles, iron and steel and machinery. Capital goods. Japan was also building an Empire in Asia to gain raw materials and political power.
4	1930 to 1950	Efficient production of a wider range of goods including metals and chemicals. Most factories destroyed in the Second World War.
5	1950 to present	Advanced technology and mass production of cars, ships and consumer goods such as TVs, video recorders and cameras. Mass consumption at home and on world markets. All serviced by an efficient tertiary sector.

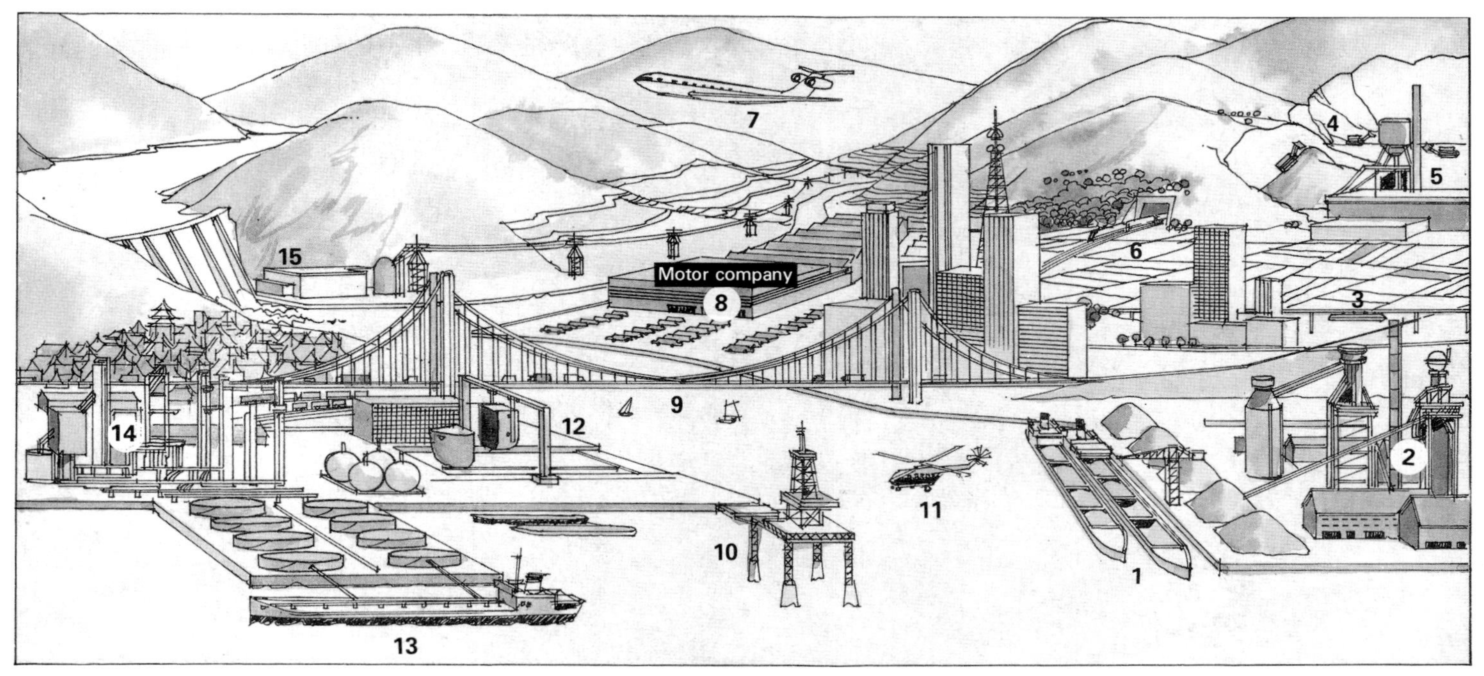

22 Sketch showing Mitsubishi products

FOLLOW-UP WORK

1 Study the network (20). How does each of these factors help the growth of industry:
(a) farming, (b) people saving money, (c) trade?

2 Study the triangular graph (23). Points have been plotted to show the types of jobs people had for each of the years 1880, 1930 and 1980.
(a) Which year does each of the letters A, B and C on the graph represent?
(b) On your own copy of the graph, mark points for 1960, 1970 and 1988. Use the statistics in table (19).

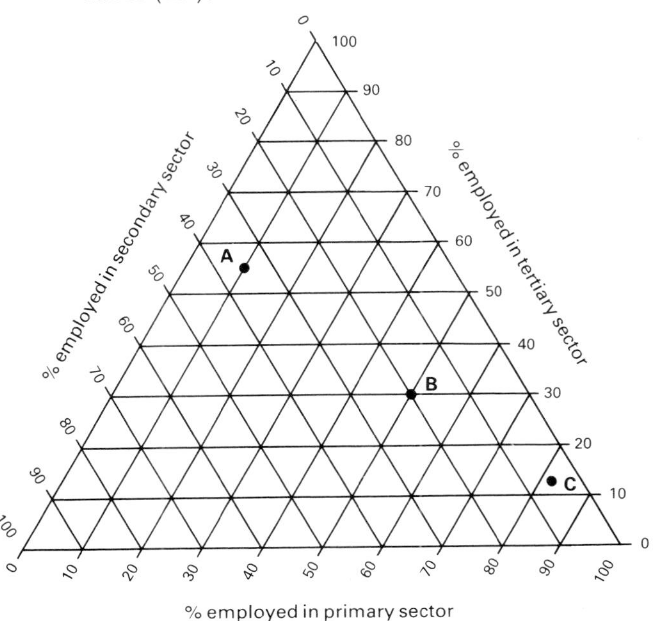

23 Triangular graph

(c) What change occurred in the structure of employment between 1880 and 1988?

3 Why did Japan concentrate on producing capital goods in the earlier years and consumer goods in more recent years?

4 What advantages do large companies, such as Mitsubishi, have for each of these:
(a) assembling raw materials for manufacture,
(b) mass production,
(c) selling products,
(d) developing new products?

5 Why is it a good idea for companies to make many products rather than one product?

6 Study the sketch of Mitsubishi operations (22). Describe the series of links between
(a) numbers 4, 5, 8, and 15
(b) numbers 1, 2, 10, 13 and 14.

CAPITAL AND CONSUMER GOODS

Capital goods are raw materials, semi-manufactures and manufactured items which are used to make other articles.
Consumer goods are manufactured articles which are bought and used by people and later replaced.

INDUSTRIAL GIANTS

The growth of industry in Japan centred on large companies can be experienced by playing the Industrial Giants game. Ask for details.

The steel industry

The steel industry has been at the heart of Japan's industrial growth. Steel has been used for buildings, bridges, railways, cars, ships, machinery and a wide range of consumer products for sale in Japan and overseas. The growth of the steel industry since 1950 is shown in table (24) and the main uses for steel in table (25). Present output is the second largest in the world after the USSR. Thirty per cent of the steel is exported.

24 Steel production, 1950–85

Year	*Steel production (million tonnes)*
1950	5
1955	9
1960	22
1965	41
1970	93
1975	102
1980	111
1985	105

25 How steel is used

Steel users	*% of total (1986)*
Construction, e.g. buildings and bridges	25
Vehicles, e.g. cars and lorries	19
Electrical machinery	5
Shipbuilding	4
Containers	4
General machinery	3
Home appliances, office machines	2
Dealers	33
Others	5

26 Raw material imports by source, 1986

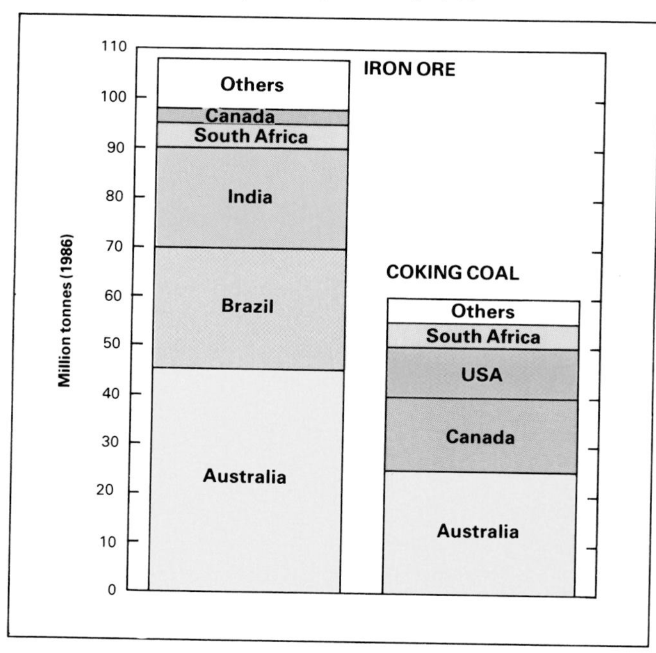

Japan almost completely lacks the raw materials for the steel industry. Imports provide 99.7 per cent of the iron ore, 96 per cent of the coking coal and all the crude oil that is needed. The compound bar graphs (26) show the main suppliers. Only 8 per cent of steel scrap is imported as there are large supplies from Japan's own cities.

Study map (27) which shows where the main steelworks are located.

A modern steelworks

The Oita steelworks opened in 1971 (27). It was built on flat land reclaimed from the sea (28). Study the photograph and the plan of the works (29). It is called an integrated steelworks because all the stages in making a sheet of steel take place on one site. The diagram shows how the industry operates as a system with inputs, processes, output and feedback. The maps, photograph and diagram help to explain the site and location of steelworks in Japan.

27 Location of steelworks

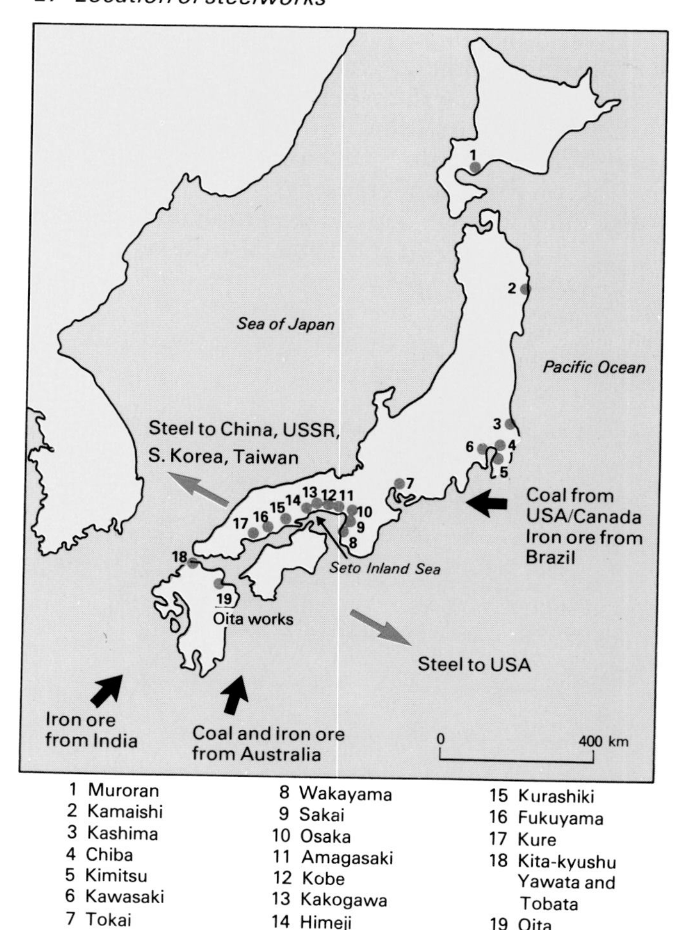

1 Muroran
2 Kamaishi
3 Kashima
4 Chiba
5 Kimitsu
6 Kawasaki
7 Tokai
8 Wakayama
9 Sakai
10 Osaka
11 Amagasaki
12 Kobe
13 Kakogawa
14 Himeji
15 Kurashiki
16 Fukuyama
17 Kure
18 Kita-kyushu Yawata and Tobata
19 Oita

SITE AND LOCATION

The site is the spot where the factory is built. The location is where the factory is placed in relation to the area around it. Factors affecting the choice of a location include access to raw materials, labour supply and markets.

FOLLOW-UP WORK

1 Using the statistics in table (24), draw a line graph to show steel production from 1950 to 1985. Use a scale of 10 million tonnes per cm on the vertical axis. What does your graph show?

2 Draw a compound bar graph similar to (26) to show steel exports in 1986. Use these statistics.

Total 30 million tonnes

China	9	Taiwan	2	Hong Kong	1
USA	4	Indonesia	1	Others	6
USSR	2.5	India	1		
S. Korea	2.5	Thailand	1		

Why is Japan in a good location in the world to supply these countries with steel? Use an atlas for this exercise.

3 Study map (27), map (65) on page 62 and the graph and systems diagram on these pages. Suggest four reasons why steelworks are located on the south coast of Japan.

4 Copy plan (29) of the steelworks.
(a) Draw arrows to show the movement from raw materials to finished product.
(b) What advantages are there in the layout of the steelworks?
(c) Why was the steelworks built on reclaimed land?
(d) What advantages of the site are shown on the photograph and plan?

WORLD STEEL

Which countries produce most steel? Why is the pattern of world steel production changing? Ask for the information and exercise sheet.

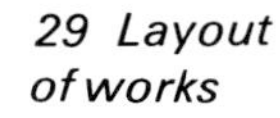

29 Layout of works

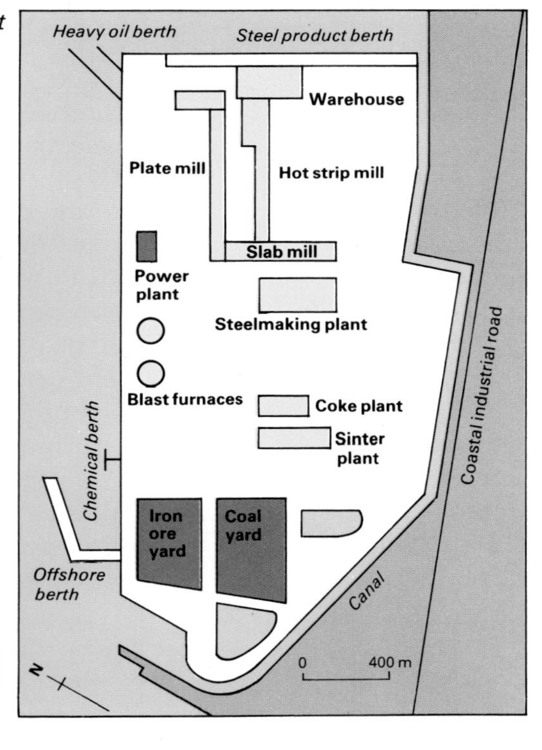

28 Oita steelworks

30 Industry as a system: steel production at Oita, 1986

Shipbuilding: adapting to change

Japan has made half of all the tonnage of ships sailing in the world today. Huge oil tankers, bulk-carriers, general cargo ships and container ships made in Japanese shipyards help to carry the products of world trade. Japan needed many of these ships to carry raw materials from other countries to supply her growing industries and for the export of manufactured products to world markets.

31 Nissei Maru *oil tanker*

No other form of transport can carry large quantities of goods as cheaply as ships. Large shipyards were built in the 1970s to make giant-sized ships to reduce the cost of transporting bulky products such as iron ore, coal and petroleum (31). Photograph (32) shows the section-joining yard at the Ariake shipyard which opened in 1973. Map (33) shows where all the big shipyards are located. Compare this map with map (27) which shows the location of steelworks. Shipbuilding is a heavy industry which uses huge amounts of steel. The line graph (34) shows the rapid growth of shipbuilding

32 Ariake shipyard

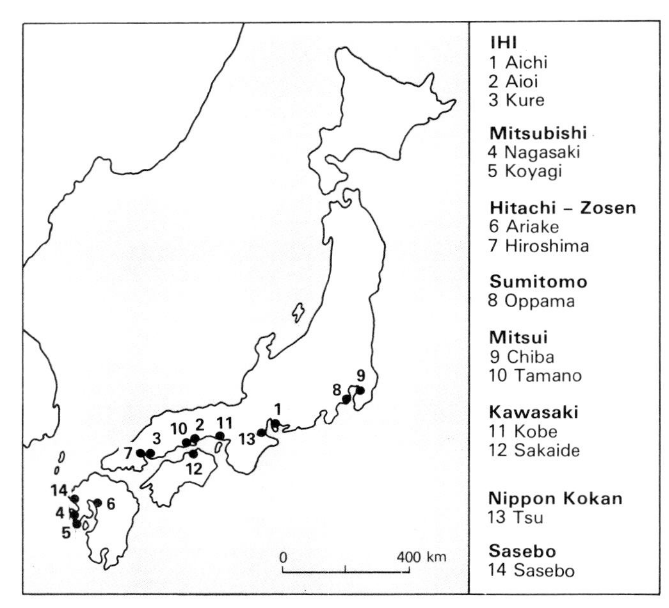

33 Main shipyards in Japan

in Japan until 1975 when a decline began. The pie graphs (35) show the countries which made most ships in the peak year 1975, and in 1987, which was a year of low output. These are the reasons why shipbuilding declined in Japan.

- In 1973, the countries which produce oil increased their prices and reduced the amount of oil for sale. Industrial countries in Europe, North America and also Japan, which depended on cheap oil imports, went into an industrial recession; there was less trade and less need for new ships.

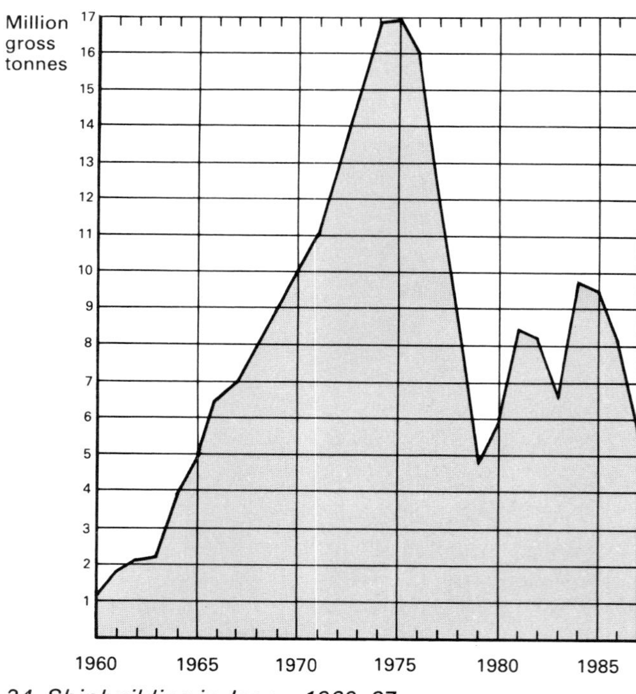

34 Shipbuilding in Japan, 1960–87

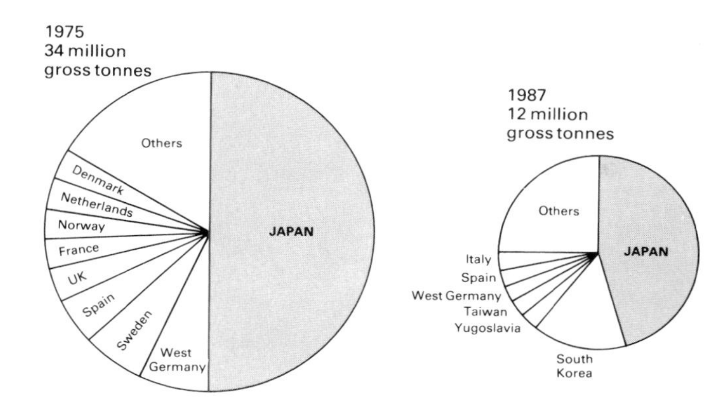

35 World shipbuilding, 1975 and 1987

- Big new ships built in the 1960s and early 1970s replaced old ones. Fewer new ships were needed after this time.
- There was competition from newly industrialised countries such as South Korea, Taiwan and Brazil, which make big ships at a low cost.
- The value of Japanese money (yen) increased compared with the US dollar. Income from the sale of ships is in dollars but payment for labour and materials is in yen. The result is that Japan can no longer make ships for a low price.

These are some of the ways in which Japan is trying to solve the problem of a declining industry.

1 Closure of shipyards.
2 Movement of people to more profitable parts of the company.
3 Combination of shipbuilding operations, and sharing of orders.
4 Design of new high-performance ships for specialist markets.
5 Manufacture of new products, e.g. oil platforms and floating industrial platforms (36, 37).
6 Setting up of new businesses in shipbuilding towns. Hotels, sport and leisure facilities are examples.

36 An industrial platform: a pulp mill made in Japan and floated to the Amazon forest in Brazil

37 A big shipyard without ships

FOLLOW-UP WORK

1 Briefly describe how a big oil tanker like the one in photograph (32) is made.
2 Describe and suggest reasons for the location of shipyards as shown on map (33).
3 Suggest two reasons why the raising of oil prices in 1973 caused a decline in the demand for new oil tankers.
4 Study the pie graphs (35).
 (a) How much less tonnage of ships was launched in 1987 as compared with 1975?
 (b) Which country is Japan's biggest competitor?
5 The decline of shipbuilding has caused unemployment in other industries as well as at the shipyards. How can you explain this?
6 Why do most people in shipbuilding towns suffer when shipyards close?
7 Study photograph (37).
 (a) What evidence is there that large ships can be built at this shipyard?
 (b) What two products, mentioned on this page, are being made at points A and B?
8 Which of the six ways to solve the problem of the declining shipbuilding industry will be most welcomed by people who live in shipbuilding towns?

BUYING THE WORLD'S RESOURCES

Japan lacks the fuel and raw materials for manufacturing industry. The ships built there help to carry these resources to Japan from all parts of the world. Ask for the exercise sheet.

> *HEAVY INDUSTRY*
>
> The manufacture of bulky products using large amounts of steel and other materials. Shipbuilding and the manufacture of heavy machinery are heavy industries.

The car industry

Japan has the largest motor vehicle industry in the world producing over 12 million vehicles every year. The graph (38) shows that just a few countries, including Japan, make most of the vehicles which have revolutionised transport throughout the world this century.

The statistics in table (39) show how recently and how rapidly the car industry has grown in Japan. Car exports numbered only *two* in 1955 but 4.5 million in 1987. The shipbuilding industry designs and makes car transporters which can carry 6000 cars to world markets (40).

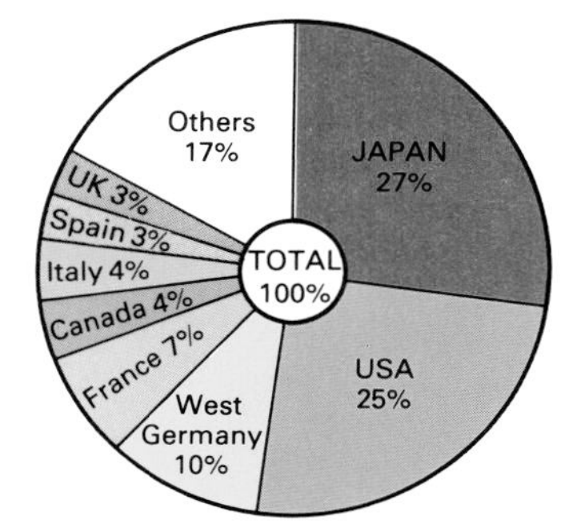

38 Motor vehicle production 1986

39 Japan: car output and exports, 1950–87

Year	*Car output*	*Car exports*
1950	1 594	7
1955	20 268	2
1960	165 094	7 013
1965	696 176	100 716
1970	3 178 708	725 586
1975	4 567 854	1 827 286
1980	7 038 108	3 947 160
1985	7 646 816	4 426 762
1987	7 891 087	4 507 714

40 Loading cars into a car carrier

Motor vehicle manufacture is a key industry in Japan employing 5 million people either directly in factories or indirectly in sales and transport. Vehicle sales provide 12 per cent of all the income from manufacturing industry, which is second only to the electrical equipment industry.

Toyota is Japan's largest motor vehicle company making 30 per cent of Japan's vehicles. The company began in 1926, making textile looms in Nagoya. The first cars were made at one end of the loom works in 1933. In 1935, the first car factory was opened at Koromo (later renamed Toyota) where there was space for building large car factories (41). The location of Toyota city is shown on map (42).

In 1987 Toyota made 2.7 million cars and 1 million trucks and buses. Half of these were sold in Japan and half were exported. The company employs 65 000 people, mainly in five huge assembly plants and six component factories in Toyota City.

41 Car assembly plant

42 Location of Toyota car works

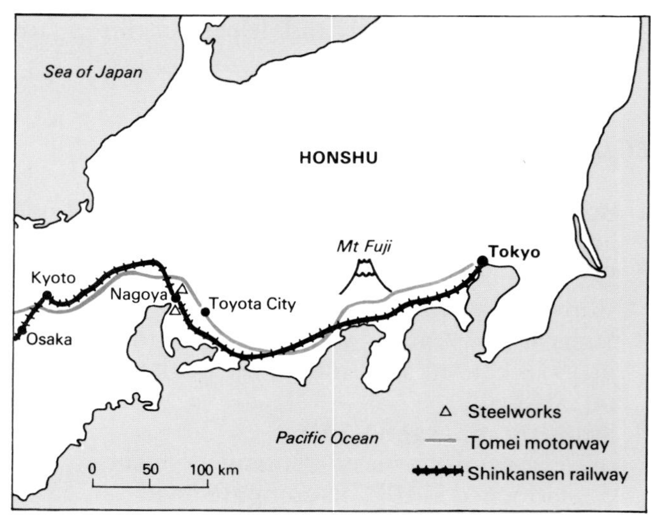

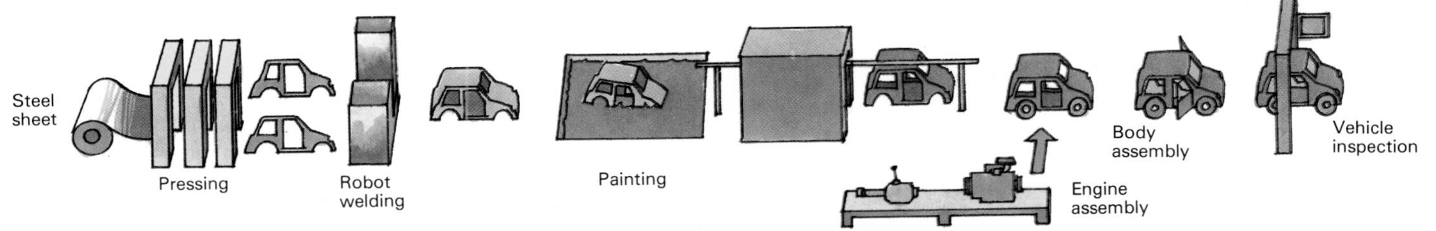

43 Stages in making a car

44 Car assembly

45 Robot welding

ASSEMBLY INDUSTRY

An industry where products are made on an assembly line (43) with men (44) and robots (45) putting together components (parts) manufactured in other factories. Parts are standardised, allowing mass production of a single product, such as a car or truck, at the lowest cost possible.

46 Markets for Japanese cars, 1987

Area	%
North America	55
Europe	31
Asia	7
Oceania	3
Central America	2
Africa	1
South America	1

FOLLOW-UP WORK

1 Draw line graphs for Japanese car output and exports between 1950 and 1987. Use the statistics in table (39) and a scale of 2 cm for 1 million cars on the vertical axis. Use your graphs to help with these:
   (a) In which fifteen-year period did the car industry grow at the fastest rate?
   (b) Was the proportion of total car output that was exported greatest in the 1970s or the 1980s?
2 Study the figures of car exports (46).
   (a) Suggest reasons why North America and Europe are the biggest markets.
   (b) Suggest reasons why people in the UK and the USA buy Japanese cars rather than home-produced cars.
   (c) How will this affect the local car industries?
   (d) Why is Japan well-placed to export cars to Asia and Oceania?
   (e) Suggest reasons why few cars are exported to Africa and South America.
3 What is meant by the following terms:
   (a) mass production, (b) assembly line,
   (c) components, (d) robot welders?
4 Why do car factories (41) need plenty of space?
5 Copy diagram (47), making each of the seven boxes larger on your diagram. Into each box write facts and figures which you can find in the text, maps and photographs. Which are the most important factors?

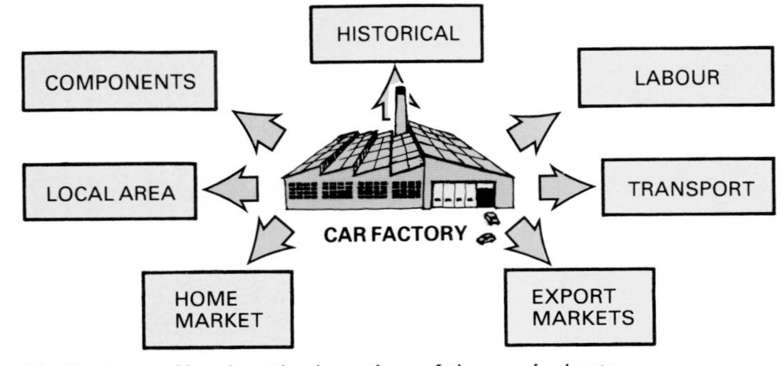

47 Factors affecting the location of the car industry

Electronics: the importance of people

Since the Second World War the electronics industry has grown rapidly in Japan. The 1960s was a boom period for household electrical appliances. There was a huge market to supply in Japan, USA, UK and many countries in Europe. These are labour-intensive industries which were ideal for Japan with a large and skilful labour force. Hitachi is the largest employer with 161 000 workers in factories and research centres located in the south-east near power, routeways and markets (48).

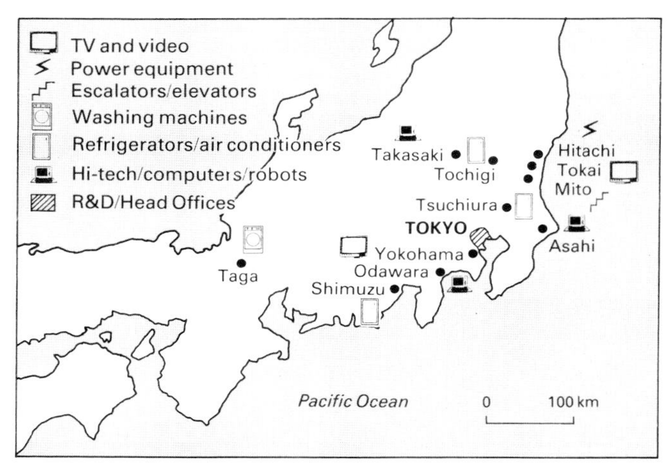

48 *Location of Hitachi factories*

Hitachi began in 1910 as an electrical repair shop making electric motors for a copper mine. The company became more diversified as knowledge and techniques were transferred from one activity to another to meet the demands of the time – power and industrial equipment from the 1950s to the 1960s, consumer products from the 1960s to 1970s and electronics and information systems in the 1980s. The company now spends 2 billion US dollars every year and employs 16 000 people on research and development (R&D) to provide new products for the consumers of the 1990s, bringing changes to our everyday lives (49).

49 *R & D*

The statistics (50) and graph (51) show how and why the demand for some household electrical goods is rising rapidly whilst demand for others has levelled out.

Japan has become one of the world's most prosperous advanced industrial countries. Wages and the value of the yen are high. Newly industrialised countries (NICs) which surround Japan have lower wages and a less valuable currency. These countries can make colour television sets, radios and video cassettes, for example, at a lower cost than Japan. Japanese

50 *Proportion of homes in Japan owning consumer durables, 1987*

Product	*% of homes*
Colour TV sets	99
Washing machines	99
Refrigerators	98
Vacuum cleaners	98
Stereos	59
Air conditioners	57
Microwave ovens	52
Videocassette recorders (VCRs)	43
Push-button phones	20
Personal computers	12
CD players	10

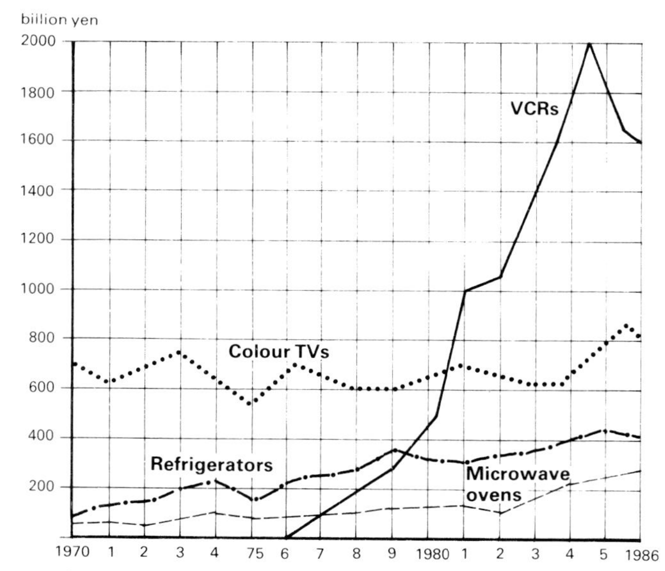

51 *Output of household electrical goods in Japan, 1970–86*

companies have set up factories in South Korea, Taiwan, Singapore and Hong Kong, for example, to take advantage of these low costs of production which include low-cost labour, cheap land, low taxes and government help. Diagram (52) shows that Japan is the industrial core, and offshore countries are the periphery.

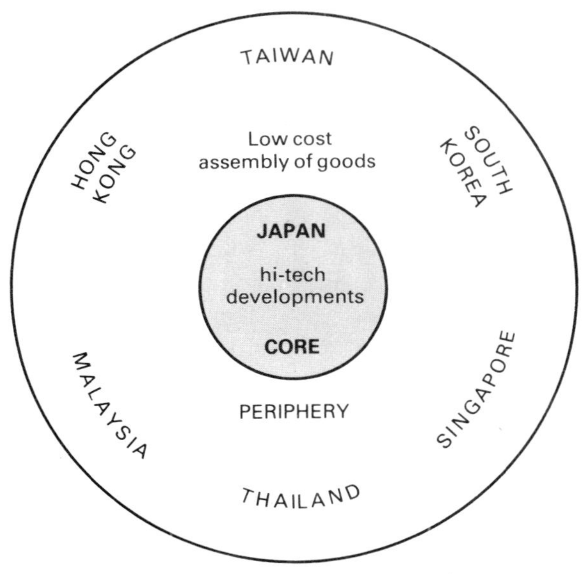

52 The core-periphery industrial model

> *CORE AND PERIPHERY*
>
> The core is the long-established industrial centre of operations which has the ability to research and develop new products.
> The periphery is the area located away from the core where well-tried industries can be set up to use low-cost labour supplies.

53 Making Sony TVs in South Wales

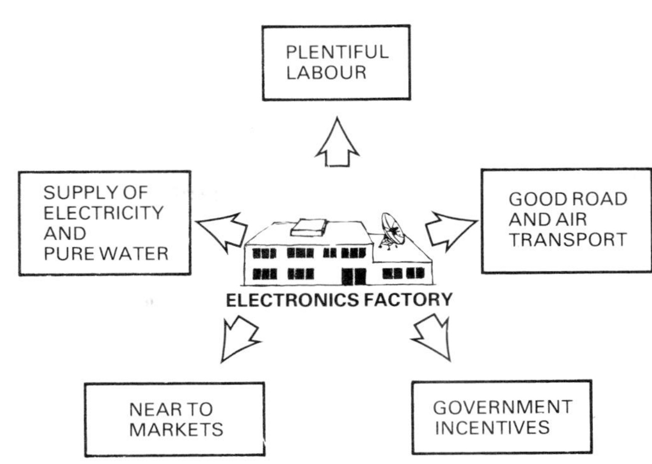

54 Location of an electronics factory

Japan now finds it profitable to locate factories in the main markets of the USA, UK and Europe. There are twenty-one Japanese electronics factories in the UK employing 14 000 people, often in areas like South Wales where unemployment levels are high. Hitachi makes colour TVs and microwave ovens in Aberdare, and Sony makes colour TVs at Bridgend (53).

We have seen that electronics industries can be located where costs are lowest at the time. They can be closed at one location and opened somewhere else in a short space of time. They are not fixed to locations like the shipbuilding industry. They are called 'footloose' industries. Compare the location diagram (54) with your car industry diagram (47).

FOLLOW-UP WORK

1 Which of the products in table (50) do you have at home? How many are made in Japan?
2 Why are Japanese companies likely to make more computers than washing machines in the next few years?
3 Why has Hitachi added a new range of products to its output every ten years since the 1960s?
4 Why do big companies like Hitachi spend huge sums of money on research and development every year?
5 Why do Japanese companies make electrical goods in
   (a) Taiwan and South Korea,
   (b) USA and Britain?
6 What advantages and disadvantages might these factories have for Britain?
7 Why might the NICs find that Japan closes their factory in the future and opens one in a different country?
8 Why are people more important than materials in the electronics industry? (Compare with the steel industry, for example.)

Industrial pollution

Japan's industrial growth occurred very quickly and many large oil refineries, chemical works, steelworks, paper mills and shipyards were built on the coast (55). These were densely settled areas and the factories attracted more people. The land between Tokyo and Kobe became the most crowded area in the world, with factories and houses tightly packed together. The factories let out smoke into the air and waste into the rivers and sea. Clean air and fresh water began to disappear. Tests on water near to large factories, as shown in photograph (56), found heavy pollution. People did not complain, because they were loyal to their company and country. Then came the tragedy of Minamata Bay.

Minamata is a fishing town on the island of Kyushu. In 1953, fish and shellfish were landed dead in catches from the bay. Cats in the area began to die in large numbers. People in the town began to lose their vision and sense of hearing; their speech became slurred and their lips, hands and feet became numb. These are the symptoms of mercury poisoning. The Chisso chemical factory at Minamata had been putting waste mercury into the sea. Bacteria in the water converted the mercury into a poison called methyl-mercury. This poison was taken in by plankton. Fish eat plankton, and they absorbed the mercury. The diet of the local fishermen and their families is mainly fish. Mercury waste from the factory had found its way into the tissues of the body, including the brain.

Eight thousand people were affected, including babies born with brain damage. By 1988, 750 people had died from the disease which is named after their town. In 1979, two former executives of the Chisso company were found guilty, in court, of allowing mercury to be discharged into the sea which had led to death and disease in Minamata.

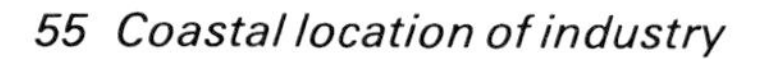

55 Coastal location of industry

56 Water pollution tests

The pollution of Minamata Bay and the disaster that followed is one example of many shown on the map on page 59. The delicate balance between living things and the environment has been disturbed on a massive scale.

The number of people suffering pollution diseases increases each year. The statistics in table (57) were the most serious cases in 1988.

57 Pollution diseases, 1988

Pollution disease	*Number of people*
Air pollution diseases including chronic bronchitis and asthma	95 000
Minamata disease	7 330
Itai-itai disease	54
Chronic arsenic poisoning	110

FOLLOW-UP WORK

1 Draw a diagram or a series of diagrams to show the chain of events which led to the death of people in Minamata from mercury poisoning.
2 Study the map on page 59. Make a list of the different ways factories cause pollution.
3 Why are large numbers of people affected by pollution in Japan?
4 Why will the new electronics industries cause less pollution than the old heavy industries?

POLLUTION

Ask for the worksheet on pollution.

Toyama. People living downstream from a lead and cadmium mine began to suffer from leg and back pains. The problem began in 1945 when drinking water was taken from the river. People eating rice from paddyfields near the mine also became ill. The cause was cadmium poisoning from polluted water. The resulting disease makes the bones brittle and deforms the skeleton. It is called itai-itai (ouch-ouch) disease because it is very painful. By 1988, 149 people had suffered from the disease, of whom 95 had died.

Niigata. A chemical factory was found to be putting waste mercury in the Agana River in 1965. By 1988, 723 people had suffered from Minamata disease, of whom 173 had died.

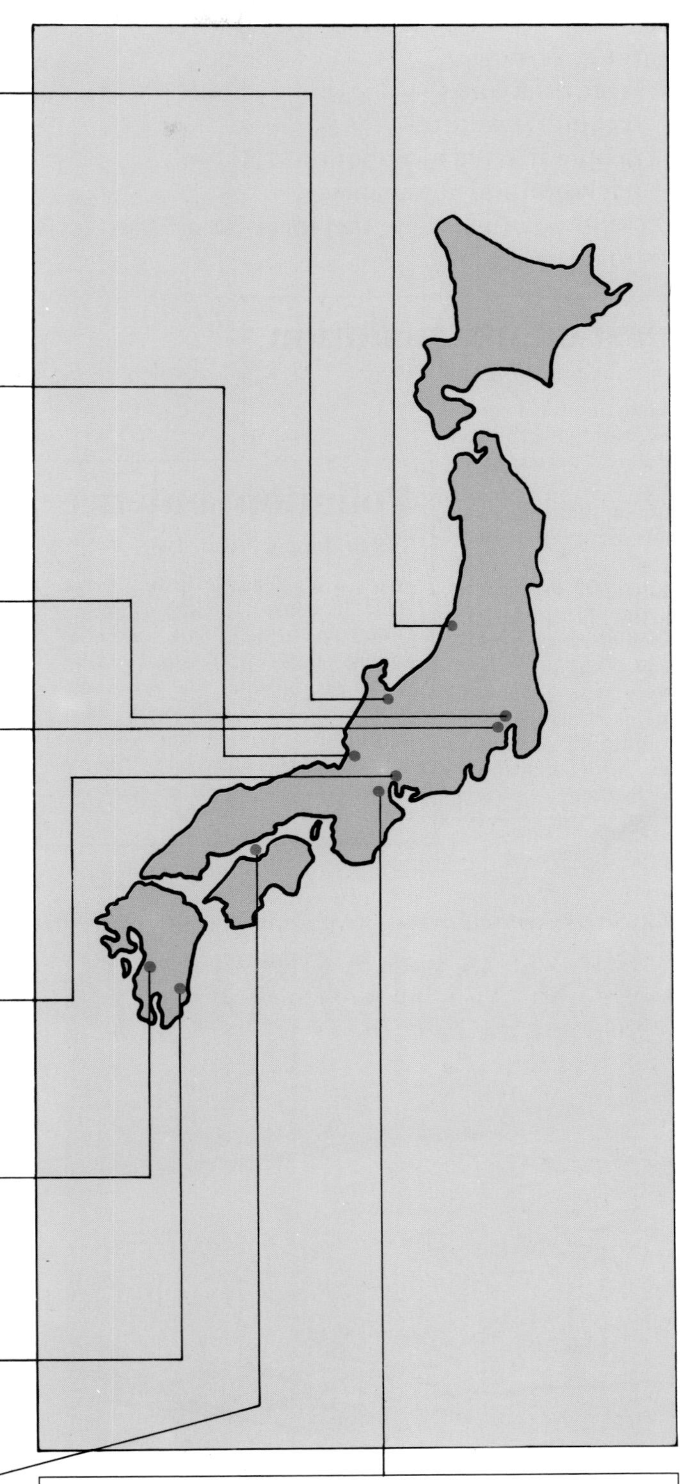

Tsuruga. In 1981, radio-active water overflowed the uranium tank at the nuclear power station. Fifty-six men were exposed to radiation and contaminated water flowed into the sea.

Tokyo. Air and water pollution are at a serious level. Cyanide discharged into the River Tama by a steelworks was discovered a few hours before it would have been taken into the city's water supply.

Kawasaki. Huge steelworks and chemical factories let out smoke and chemicals into the air. There are severe outbreaks of Yokkaichi asthma (see below).

Nagoya. Air pollution is caused by chemical and engineering companies. In 1972, 1500 people were treated in hospital for the effects of fumes. There is no life in the rivers or the bay.

Minamata. Mercury poisoning started in 1953. Minamata disease is a painful, blinding and paralysing illness.

Miyazaki. In 1971, people living near the Toroku mine began to suffer from arsenic poisoning. Water had been affected by arsenic dumps at the mine. By 1988, 102 people were ill; 34 had died.

Seto Inland Sea. There is heavy pollution of these still waters by factories, houses and oil tankers. Red tides of algae occur and beaches are polluted.

Yokkaichi. Fumes from petrochemical works have caused acute asthma in thousands of people. It is known as Yokkaichi asthma. Ise Bay is very polluted.

Discuss ways in which the problem of industrial pollution can be tackled. Study the photographs and newspaper reports on this page. Consider the action that could be taken by the following:

- the government
- large companies
- technical institutes
- people affected by pollution
- television and newspapers
- banks
- schools

Present your ideas in the form of a letter to a national newspaper.

Protest on fish pollution

Minamata, Japan, 20 Aug. 1973

The Chisso chemical company suspended production today because a fishermen's blockade has stopped supplies of raw materials for the past two weeks.

About 5,000 fishermen began the blockade to back demands that the company should pay 14.850m yen (about £22.2m) as compensation for polluting fishing grounds with industrial waste. – Reuter

Pollution sentence

Tokyo, Japan, 3 Mar. 1988

After a legal battle lasting more than 30 years, Japan's Supreme Court has upheld jail sentences against leaders of a company who were responsible for poisoning thousands of people with mercury, thus opening the way for compensation claims by victims of Minamata disease, or by relatives of the dead.

58 Waste water treatment plant

59 Smoke emission tests at Nagasaki Technical Institute

60 Flue gas treatment at Nagasaki power station

National parks: protect or develop

Most people live in cities in the south of Japan. Seventy-two per cent of the country is mountains, covered with forest. This remains in its natural wild state, undisturbed by the growth of cities and factories. A large part of this land is national park (61). The parks include mountains, lakes, waterfalls, volcanoes, hot springs and beautiful stretches of coastline.

A large number of people visit the parks. The Fuji National Park, near Tokyo, with its sacred Mount Fuji, is visited by 80 million people every year. Photograph (62) shows skiers in the Japan Alps National Park near Toyama.

A few parks are fully protected from developments, but in most parks developments can take place if they are allowed by the Environment Agency.

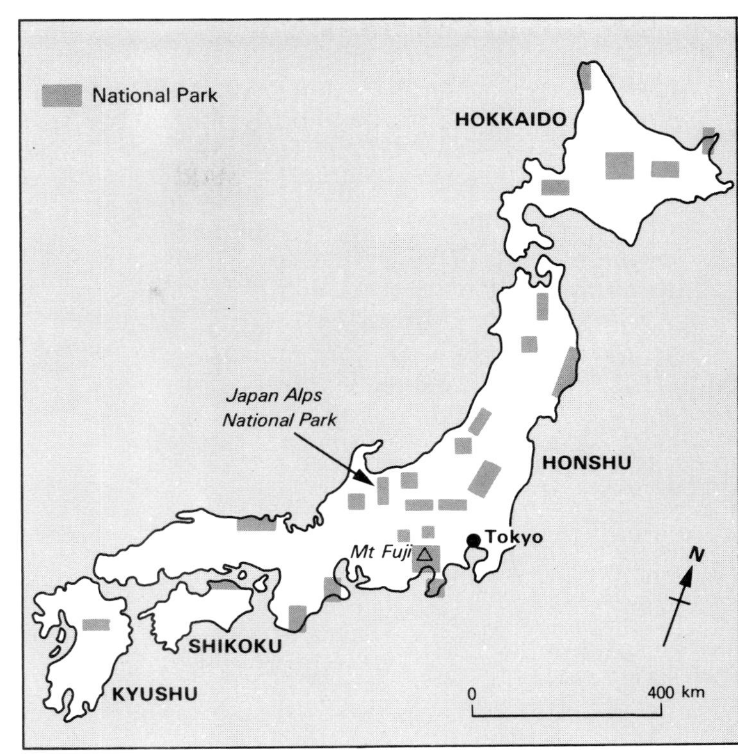

61 *National parks*

62 *Skiing in the Japan Alps*

FOLLOW-UP WORK

The Environment Agency has arranged a meeting to discuss four applications for developments in the Japan Alps National Park.

1 *The Forest Agency* Permission to use the forest on the lower slopes. The trees will be used in a new pulp and paper mill on the coast. Fast-growing pine trees will be planted each year. The scheme will help to reduce the large-scale import of wood, pulp and paper.

2 *A company recreation scheme* Permission to build a ski-lift on the upper mountain slopes. A motel will also be built, in traditional style to blend with the scenery. These will be holiday facilities for the workers at a very large car company.

3 *Ministry of power* Permission to build a dam across a mountain stream, to supply a hydro-electric power station. Development is needed to reduce the amounts of oil and coal that are imported each year.

4 *A mining company* Permission to mine copper ore which has been discovered in the park. Ore mined at the site will be taken to the company's own smelters on the south coast. A few pleasantly designed houses will be needed for the miners. This development will cut the cost of imported copper for Japan's electrical industries.

Discuss each scheme. Which developments will you allow? Write about the decisions you make.

The growth of cities: Tokyo

Three-quarters of the people of Japan live and work in cities. There are eleven cities with over 1 million people, and these are listed in table (63). Tokyo is the largest city with over 12 million people in the inner core and outer suburbs combined.

63 Population of the largest cities, 1987

City	*Number of people (million)*
Tokyo (23 wards)	8.2
Yokohama	3.1
Osaka	2.5
Nagoya	2.1
Sapporo	1.6
Kyoto	1.5
Kobe	1.4
Fukuoka	1.1
Kawasaki	1.1
Kitakyushu	1.0
Hiroshima	1.0

Most cities began as castle towns in the seventeenth century when the country was ruled by Tokugawa, a powerful war-lord. Each coastal plain and inland basin was ruled by a lord. Tokugawa controlled 300 of these lords from Edo (later called Tokyo). Each lord built a castle to control his province. They were built at the centre of the plain or at a river crossing or harbour. Each castle town was linked to Edo by road. The busiest road, called the Tokaido, linked Kyoto to Edo.

The emperor returned to power in 1868. Japan began to develop industries and people moved from their farms into factories in the cities. Modern industrial growth has occurred since 1960. Young

64 Bullet train on the Tokaido line

people have gone to live in the Tokaido Belt along the route of the old Tokaido road where there is now a motorway and fast railway (64). The cities and routes are shown on map (65).

Today half of Japan's 122 million people live in the Tokaido Belt, making this the most densely settled piece of land in the world. Tokyo is the capital city, largest city and biggest centre for industry, business, transport and communications. Most national and international companies in Japan want an office there. The city has grown at such a fast rate that overcrowding here has become the worst in the world. Looking down from an aircraft over the city centre (66), you can see tall office blocks and crowded streets. There is so little space that roads are built on top of buildings (67). There are underground railways and shopping areas. New offices, shops and housing areas are being built on land reclaimed from Tokyo Bay.

Photograph (68) shows that there is no space for

65 Cities and transport links

66 *Central Tokyo*

67 *Road on top of buildings*

68 *Built-up landscape in Tokyo*

parks and gardens. A quarter of the people live in tiny flats, share toilets and use public baths. Houses, schools and hospitals are next to noisy factories, roads and railways.

Over 1 million people enter and leave the centre of the city each day, to get to and from work. During the rush hours, electric trains run at one-minute intervals. The stations are crowded (69) and the trains carry three times more people than they should. The streets of the city are narrow. There are traffic jams in the rush hour on the urban motorways, so three-quarters of the commuters choose to come to work on public transport. Exhaust fumes from cars become so bad that policemen on duty wear masks and take breaths of oxygen. Checks are made on cars to make sure they are not sending out too much exhaust (70).

Map (71) shows how some of the problems of overcrowding will be improved. Large heavy industries in zone 1 will be closed and new industries opened in zone 3. Old single-storey houses will be replaced by tower blocks and parks. There will be new housing in zone 2 (72) and open spaces where children can play. Newcomers will be housed in four cities in zone 3, with factories along the radial roads and railways. The new airport at Narita is in this zone.

69 *Rush hour at a Tokyo station*

70 *Car exhaust tests*

71 *The Tokyo plan*

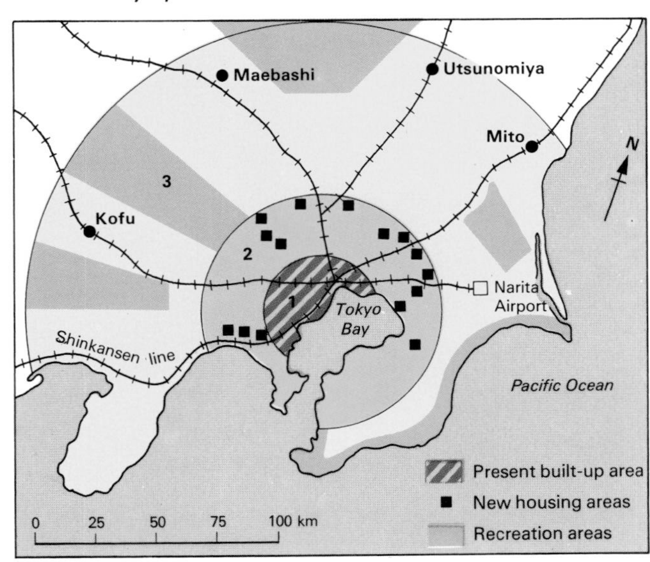

72 *New housing in zone 2*

FOLLOW-UP WORK

1 Why did castle towns make a good basis for modern cities?
2 What features shown on map (65) have helped cities to grow?
3 If a large factory is built in the Tokaido Belt, why will many small factories grow around it?
4 If a family leaves the countryside and moves to Tokyo, why does their arrival help to make jobs for even more people?
5 Draw a full-page sketch to show some of the problems of overcrowding in Tokyo. Use the photographs on pages 62 and 63 to help you.
6 Copy diagram (73) which shows how Tokyo has tried to solve the problem of overcrowding. Add two more ways in the empty boxes.
7 Study the Tokyo plan (71).
  (a) Why will it be better to live in zone 2 than in zone 1?
  (b) Why will some factories remain in zone 1, along Tokyo Bay?
  (c) Why does the plan fail to solve the rush-hour problem?

73 *Solving the problem of overcrowding*

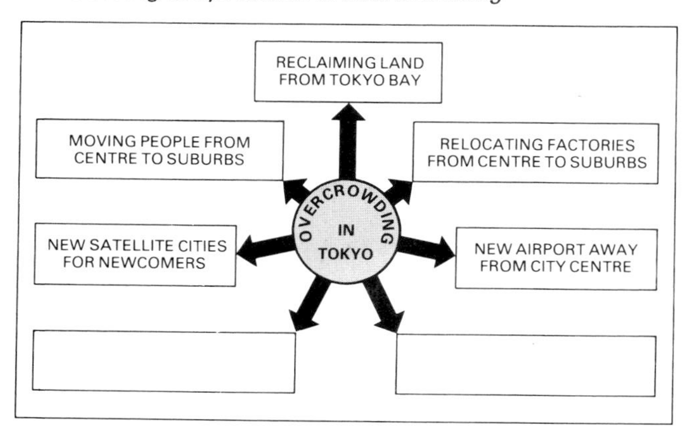

8 Shinkansen (new trunk line) railways link Tokyo to all parts of Japan. Tokaido Shinkansen is the line shown on map (65) on which 'bullet' trains reach 210 km.p.h. on the journey to Fukuoka. Study diagram (74) and the train timetable (75) and answer the questions which follow.

74 *Use of Shinkansen*

	Company business	Private business	Sightseeing
A Weekday	55%	20%	25%
B Weekend	23%	36%	41%

75 *Tokyo-Fukuoka journey times*

Leave	*Arrive*			
Tokyo	Nagoya	Osaka	Hiroshima	Fukuoka
Time 08.00	10.03	11.12	13.08	14.40
Distance in km from Tokyo	342	515	821	1069

(a) What is the main use for the railway?
(b) How does the use of the railway change at weekends?
(c) How long does the trip take from Tokyo to Fukuoka (which is the same distance as the length of Britain)?
(d) Why will businessmen find the fast train useful?

WORLD CITIES

Ask for the worksheet.

URBANISATION

The growth of towns and cities such as Tokyo. This is caused by migration from rural areas (countryside) and by the large natural increase of a youthful city population. Ask for the exercise sheet on the world's largest cities.

AGGLOMERATION

This is when a number of factories are built close to each other. They often share materials, use the same transport and other services, and serve the same market.

Conflict over land: new airports in Japan

On 27th March 1988, 4000 students marched to Tokyo's Narita Airport (71, 76) as a protest on the tenth anniversary of its opening. Eleven thousand police were there to make sure they did not storm the airport. Ten years earlier a similar army of students wrecked the airport terminal, blew up the radio tower and sabotaged the railway from the city. At the same time farmers erected steel towers near to the end of the runway to stop planes landing and taking off.

Work started on the new international airport, sixty kilometres east of Tokyo, in 1965. By 1971 the runway and buildings were ready to use but protests by farmers, supported by radical students, prevented the airport being opened until 1978.

These were the arguments for and against the new airport.

For the airport

- Tokyo airport at Haneda, near the centre of the city, could not handle the rapid increase in traffic. The airways were congested and dangerous.
- There was no space to enlarge the airport at Haneda.
- A new airport built too close to the city would cause serious noise pollution.
- There was plenty of flat land at Narita for the new airport.
- The new airport would create thousands of new jobs at Narita and along the routes to the airport from Tokyo. This would help to reverse the movement of people into the city.

Against the airport

- The airport, with its 4000-metre runway, covered some of the best arable farmland in Japan. The land had belonged to the farming families for generations and was protected by Japan's agricultural tenancy laws.
- Nobody was consulted about the new development. The land was requisitioned from the farmers.
- Narita was a quiet rural town which would be overwhelmed by the new developments. One thousand houses would need to be knocked down on the airport site.
- Pollution of the land, sea and air was on a massive scale in Japan in the 1960s and 1970s. The new airport would be another threat to the environment.
- Narita would be the most isolated international airport in the world. Huge areas of land would be lost under the motorway and railway stretching from Tokyo to the airport.

76 New Tokyo International Airport (Narita)

FOLLOW-UP WORK

1 Which are the strongest arguments for and against the new airport?
2 Would you be for or against the airport? Say why.
3 Study the drawing (77) and details below for a new airport at Osaka to serve Japan's second largest urban area from 1993. Why might this scheme cause less opposition than Narita?

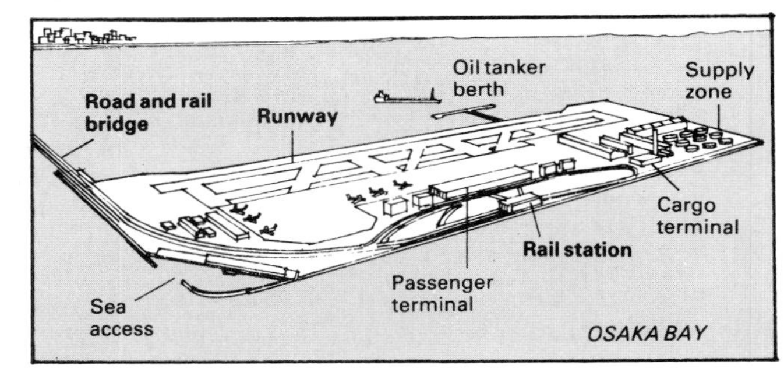

77 Artist's impression of the new airport for Osaka

Features of the new airport (Kansai)

- Built on 511 hectares of land reclaimed from Osaka Bay
- Located five kilometres off shore with access by a new bridge and by boat
- No flights over land, allowing 24-hour operations
- Compensation paid to fishermen for any loss of earnings caused by the new airport

FLIGHT PATHS FROM TOKYO TO LONDON

Ask for the worksheets.

China

1 Rice transplanting in east China

2 Mountains of south-west China

A large country with a large population

There are more than 1 billion people living in China, which is one-fifth of the people of the world. Eighty per cent of the Chinese people are farmers, who live on the fertile plains and river basins in the east of the country, shown in photograph (1). In the west of China, there are high mountains, as in photograph (2), and great deserts where few people live. Map (3) shows where most people live. Notice the differences between the west and east of China, shown on the map and in the photographs.

3 China

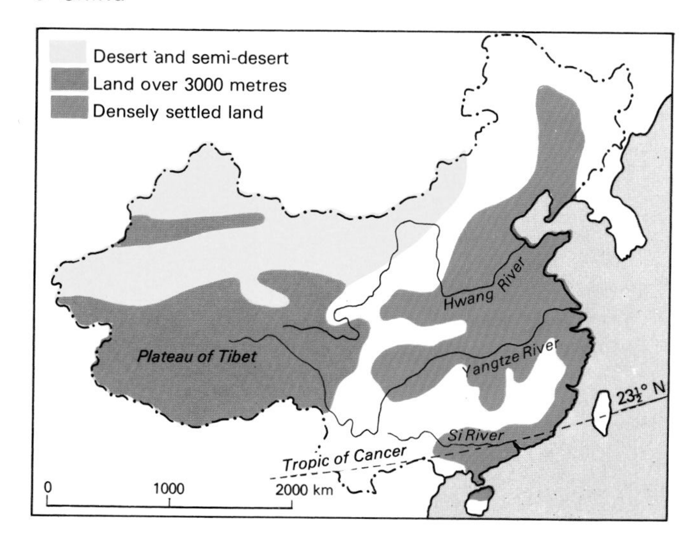

FOLLOW-UP WORK

China is the third largest country in the world, after the USSR and Canada.

1 Measure the distance across the country
   (a) west to east,
   (b) north to south.
2 Large areas of land have few people. How much of China is
   (a) mountains,
   (b) desert?
3 The best farmlands in the east are very densely settled. Describe the land, the number of people and the jobs being done in photograph (1) of rice fields of east China.

Three thousand five hundred years ago, the first written records show that there were 5 million Chinese. They lived on the North China Plain, where they had cleared the woods and drained the marshes to grow wheat and millet. Map (4) shows where they lived.

As the population increased, farmers moved south into warm, wet lands to grow crops. The settled farmers built the Great Wall of China to protect themselves from the barbaric horsemen who lived on the grasslands in the north.

By AD 1100, there were 100 million Chinese. The delta of the River Yangtze was densely settled. Very few people lived in the south, where there was thick forest, steep slopes, tropical diseases and dangerous aboriginal tribes.

The population rose to 200 million in 1760, 300 million in 1800 and 400 million in 1830. A fast-growing type of rice was grown to feed all these people.

Most of the land was owned by landlords. The poor peasants had to give half their crops as rent to the landlord and pay taxes to the government. After a bad harvest, the peasants had to borrow from the moneylender, usually the landlord, and pay interest on the loan.

A peasant had little land. A long tradition of dividing land amongst sons had resulted in tiny farms. The peasant farmer's tools were simple, his soil overworked, his seeds poor quality, and his crops often ruined by pests and diseases, drought and floods. Famines occurred every year.

Before 1949, one in every five children died from disease or starvation. Most people lived only thirty years. In 1949, the Communists set up the People's Republic of China, and began to improve health, education and living standards. With better medicines, hygiene and diet, fewer children died and people lived longer. The result has been a big rise in the number of people, seen clearly in graph (5). Photograph (6) shows young people working hard to control the rivers and improve the land. They must do this to grow enough food to feed the largest population in the world.

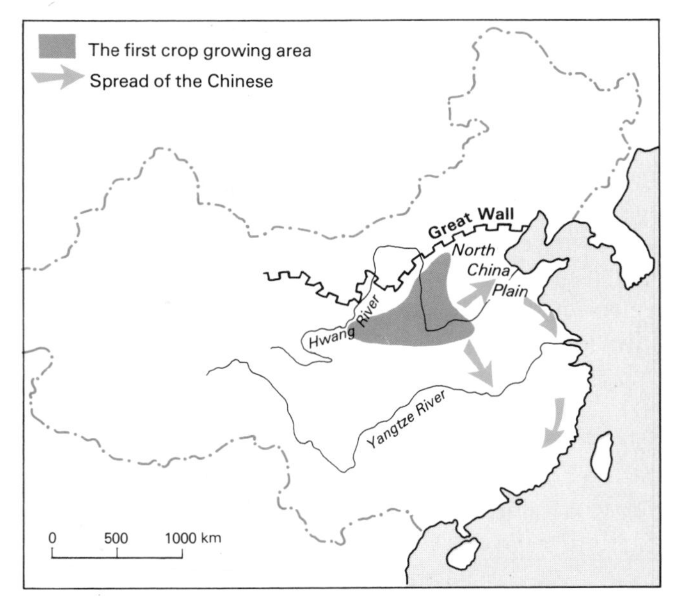

4 Spread of the Chinese

5 Population growth, 1900–90

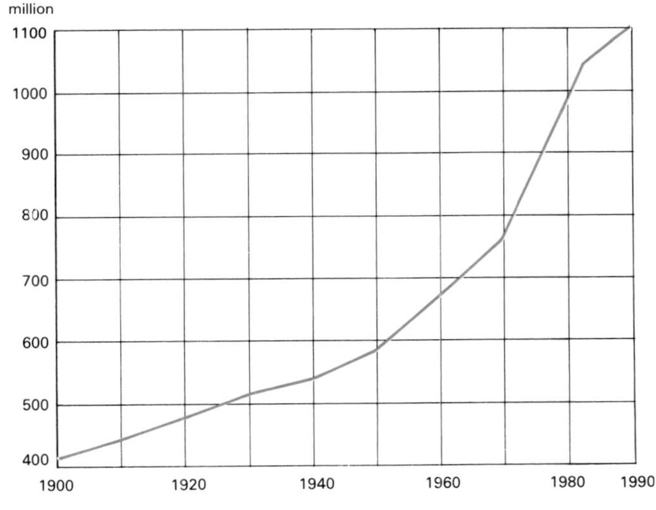

6 Young people working on a river control scheme

> *POPULATION DENSITY*
>
> The average number of people living in an area such as one square kilometre. Ask for the worksheets on population density in China and the world.

Solving the population problem

China has the world's largest population but also one-fourteenth of the world's land area. The problem is not the lack of space in which to live, but making the land provide food and resources for the huge and growing population. In 1981, there were 1000 million people in China. The birth rate was 20 per thousand and the death rate 8 per thousand. With a natural increase of 12 per thousand (1.2 per cent), the population reached 1012 million in 1982. By 1988 the number had risen to 1080 million and is expected to reach 1280 million by the end of the century. China has tried to solve the problem by different methods.

> *BIRTH RATE AND DEATH RATE*
>
> The birth rate is the number of babies born in a year for every thousand people in the country. The death rate is the number of people who died in the year per thousand people. The change in the size of the population resulting from the difference between the birth and death rates is called natural change which is a natural *increase* in almost all countries in the world.

7 Transplanting rice in south China

8 Controlling the Yellow River

FOLLOW-UP WORK

Read about three of these and answer the questions as they arise.

1 More food from the best farmland Crop yields are being increased by the use of fertilizers and pesticides. Machines can speed up farming operations (7) and allow two or more crops to be grown in one year. This is called multiple cropping. Flood control (8) and irrigation schemes regulate the flow of water to the fields and are very important in dry areas or in dry parts of the farming year.

The use of new varieties of rice and wheat to suit local conditions is part of the green revolution which has increased food production around the world.

(a) How does flood control help to increase food production?
(b) Why do quick-maturing strains of rice and wheat help to raise food production?
(c) What is the advantage of using machines on farms in China?
(d) Why is there limited demand for labour-saving machines on farms in China?

2 More farmland from mountain and desert Trees have been cut down and terraces built on steep slopes to make flat land to grow crops (9). In the dry north-west, trees have been planted to stop sand blowing across land which can be farmed.

(a) Terraces might cause as many problems as they solve. Say why.
(b) Farmers are helped most when trees are planted rather than when they are cut down. Say why.
(c) From a study of the statistics in table (10), say whether food production has increased more by increasing output from the best farmland or by extending production into less favoured areas.

9 Terraced hillside

10 Chinese farming: inputs and outputs

	1950	*1985*
Land farmed (m ha)	100	101
Land under forest (m ha)	72	130
Irrigated land (% of total)	26	52
Grain output (m tonnes)	160	379
Grain output (kg/person)	238	380
Rice yield (tonnes/ha)	2.3	4.9
Chemical fertilizer used (m tonnes)	1	13

3 Small families In 1979, China began a family planning programme with the target of one child for each married couple and a stable population (no growth) by the year 2000. This was followed in 1980 by a marriage law which set the minimum age for marriage at 20 for women and 22 for men. Billboards, posters, television and local committee members publicise the policy constantly. Rewards for keeping to one child include free education, child allowance, better housing and larger pensions. Penalties for those having more than one child include the loss of the rewards and increased taxes. The policy has been relaxed in rural areas where labour is needed to increase food output on family farms (11).

(a) Why is birth control a better solution than increasing food production for the future welfare of the Chinese?
(b) Why is limiting family size (12) difficult to achieve?
(c) From a study of the statistics (13), say whether the policy is succeeding or not.

China eases child ban

Peking (Reuter) – China's peasants are allowed to have more than one child if the first is a daughter under a policy intended in part to stop the killing of baby girls, Mr Peng Peiyun, the Family Planning Minister, said yesterday.

"Abandonment and drowning of baby girls has not completely disappeared in China," he said. "In the countryside, peasants always want a boy. If they have got a daughter but still have a chance to have another baby, this helps stop them abandoning baby girls." China's population is 1.08 billion. About 22 million children were born last year.

11 Article in The Times*, 7th Sept. 1988*

12 A family in Nanjing

13 Population growth

Year	*Birth rate*	*Death rate*	*Natural increase*
1953	45	23	22
1970	33	15	18
1980	21	8	13
1987	17	7	10

POPULATION PYRAMIDS

These are bar graphs which show the age and sex structure of the population. A true pyramid shape results from a high birth rate and high death rate. This means there are high numbers of children but low numbers of people over 50 years old. A balanced population in a developed country has a narrow pyramid. Ask for the worksheet on population pyramids.

Feeding the world's largest population

In the past, China has suffered famines when there has been a drought or flood. Huge numbers of people have died and hungry people have eaten roots and bark from trees. Today, with flood control, irrigation, food stores and trains to carry surplus food to areas where there is a shortage, famines are less likely to happen.

China is such a vast land that when the one crop of wheat is being harvested in the cool north of China (14), a second crop of rice has already been harvested in the warm south. The rain needed for these crops is brought by the south-east monsoon winds which are shown on map (15). The north and west parts of China are drier than the south and east because they are farther from these rain-bringing winds.

Rice is the staple food for most people. A meal also includes lightly cooked vegetables, usually cabbage and beans. The cabbage may be fresh, dried, boiled, casseroled, served in soups or flavoured with sauces. There is a constant flow of vegetables from the countryside to the free markets in the towns (16). Meat is eaten two or three times a week. Fish, pigs and poultry are the main sources of protein. The meal also includes fruit and a drink of tea. China is now self-sufficient in food and people are well fed.

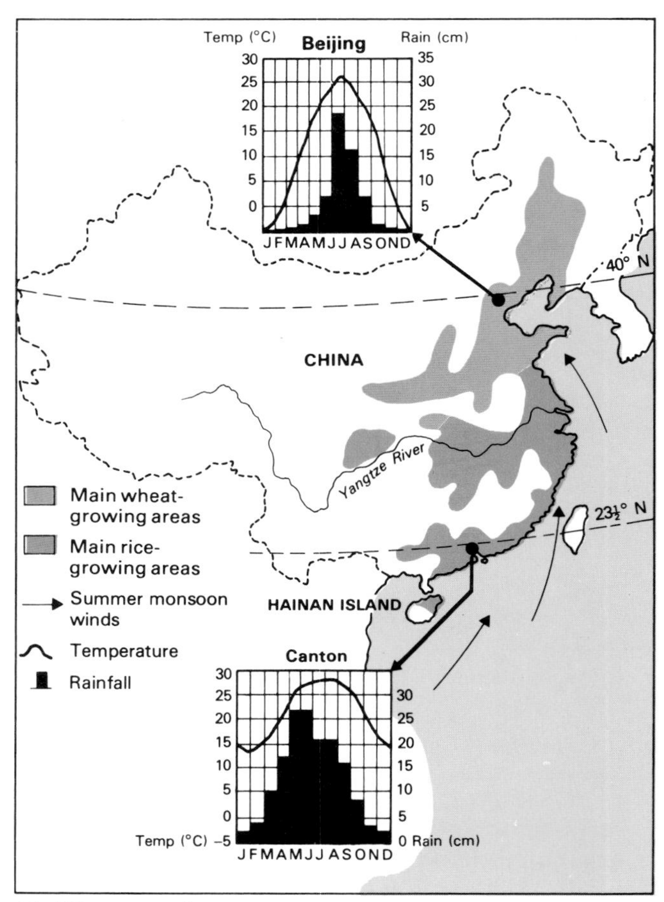

15 Climate and crops

14 Wheat harvest in north China

16 Vegetables for the town market

SELF-SUFFICIENCY

Growing enough food to meet the needs of the country's population. The degree of self-sufficiency for any product can be given as a percentage of total need. Local shortages can be met by moving food from other areas. National shortages are met by imports from other countries.

FOLLOW-UP WORK

Photograph (17) shows the main meal being cooked in a kitchen in Beijing. The lady belongs to family A or B. Study the diet of both families and answer the questions 1–5.

17 A meal in Beijing

Family A
Rice at every meal
Vegetables include cabbage, broccoli, beans, peas, bean sprouts and bamboo shoots
Main meats are pork, chicken and duck
Fish at most meals
Fruits include bananas, pineapples, lychees, mangoes, papayas, mandarins and tangerines
Locally grown tea is the main drink

Family B
Wheat ground into flour and made into noodles or steamed bread
Soybeans made into bean curd
Vegetables include cabbage, turnips, radishes, onions and garlic
Main meats are pork and chicken
Fish at some meals
Main fruits are pears and apples
Tea or boiled water is the main drink

1 (a) Which family lives in Beijing and which in Canton?
  (b) What are the reasons for your decision?
2 (a) Why are beef, lamb and milk missing from a typical Chinese meal?
  (b) Why are pork and poultry the main meats?
3 Study map (15).
  (a) Why is rice the main food crop in the south and wheat in the north of China?
  (b) Why are summer monsoon winds vital to rice farmers?
  (c) Why can farmers in the south of China grow more food than those in the north?
4 How do bicycles (16) and trains help to make sure China's large population is properly fed?

Communes: changing the system

> *COLLECTIVE FARMING*
>
> A system of farming where the land is pooled and worked together by all the families. Apart from basic rations, most food and income comes from work-points based on each person's daily contribution of work to the collective. Ask for details of the Red Dragon Commune Game in which brigades aim to reach production targets and complete big projects.

A visitor to the rice-growing lands of central and southern China can see a farming scene unchanged for generations. Photograph (18) is near Shanghai. There are scattered market towns linked to surrounding villages by waterways and narrow tracks. Most people live in the villages, which are only a couple of kilometres apart, and go out to work in the surrounding fields.

Rice farmers plough the fields, repair the low mud walls between the fields and sow seeds in nursery plots. The fields are waterlogged in the heavy summer rain. With their backs bent all day, women make bundles of rice plants to be transplanted into the paddyfields. The fields are weeded as the crop grows. At harvest time, when water has been drained from the fields, the crop is harvested with sickles, and threshed by hand.

Although the scene and the farmwork are unchanged, the life of the Chinese people has changed. In 1949, the Communist government took the land from the landowners and gave it to the people. This is called land reform. In the 1950s the people were organised into teams, brigades and communes. These are called collectives and there was a collective system of farming.

This system continued until the early 1980s. The team was made up from ten or more families who worked the land together. They were often close relatives and worked well together. A number of teams made up a brigade which included everyone in a village and surrounding hamlets. The brigade had a committee which worked out plans for the year. It bought fertilizers and machinery, sold the farm products and ran a repair shop. The brigade ran the shop (19), nursery, primary school, clinic and social centre.

Several villages made up a commune with up to 5000 households in each one. The government collected taxes from the communes and bought all the surplus food they had. The communes ran hospitals, secondary schools, mines and factories. They organised big projects such as river control schemes (6).

18 Rice-growing commune near Shanghai

19 The brigade shop

Life was very hard, right down to the ration books needed for food and clothing. Children born on the commune could expect to stay there. Each family was allowed a small plot of land on which to grow vegetables and rear pigs and poultry for their own needs.

A change in government leadership and the need to increase food output has brought big changes to the countryside since the early 1980s. The land is still communally owned but it is rented out to farming families by the collective, usually the brigade, for a period of fifteen years. This is the Responsibility System. The farmer makes a contract to produce a certain amount of grain to sell to the state and to pay taxes, after which he can grow whatever he likes to sell on a free market. Some farmers contract to produce fruit and vegetables, pigs and poultry. Small plots of land now replace the larger fields of the production teams. These will grow larger when the better farmers rent more land, set up businesses and employ people who are not doing so well. New houses, colour televisions, washing machines and refrigerators are already a sign of new prosperity in the countryside.

Local government, education and health care have passed from the commune to townships. People are still required to work on communal projects for roads, flood control and irrigation.

Many people think the new system gives farmers more incentive to produce more food. Others think the system will lead to rich and poor, landlord and labourer, which existed before 1949.

Output has risen but many say this is the result of years of good weather, better seeds, more fertilizer and using the irrigation systems built by the communes.

In 1989, demonstrations for political freedom (democracy), to match the new economic freedom, were crushed by the army.

FOLLOW-UP WORK

1 Suggest reasons why the new system
   (a) gives people more freedom,
   (b) limits the use of machinery,
   (c) works best in the best farmland areas,
   (d) does not help the one-child family policy,
   (e) might bring more varied and better-quality food.
2 Suggest reasons why many families have continued to work in a team, renting land together.

Life in the outer regions

Within the borders of China are the Han Chinese, who comprise 93 per cent of the population, and fifty-five other ethnic groups who are citizens of China but are not Chinese. The Han Chinese trace their ancestry to the Han dynasty which began in 206 BC. They share the same culture and written language and speak the same language but in hundreds of dialects. Seven per cent of the population are not Chinese but occupy half its land area (20). They live in remote mountains and pastoral and desert lands in the north and west, with completely different ways of living from the Chinese. They are often hostile to Chinese rule even though they are given some control over their own affairs.

The Tibetans

On 7th October 1950, Chinese Communist troops entered Tibet and seized control of the country. They claimed that close ties with Tibet since the seventh century made Tibet part of China. In the next thirty years the Chinese destroyed the Tibetan feudal theocracy and culture. More than a thousand Buddhist monasteries and temples were destroyed and the god-king, the Dalai Lama, fled to India after an unsuccessful uprising in 1959.

The Chinese built roads and irrigation schemes in this very dry region, set up communes, opened mines and settled half a million Han Chinese, including 50 000 soldiers, amongst the 2 million Tibetans. The main vehicles on the roads built by the Chinese (21) are army trucks. The Tibetan plateau is 5000 metres above sea level and it is too cold to grow crops. The Tibetans rear sheep, goats, yaks, cattle and horses. The herders live in yurts which are made from felt sheets strapped to a wooden framework (22). They can easily pack up and carry their yurts when they move their animals to fresh pastures.

The climate is warmer in the valleys of the plateau. The Tibetans here grow mainly barley and live a settled life in stone and brick houses (23).

Life is hard for Tibetans and they can expect to live, on average, for only forty-five years.

Since 1980, the Chinese have reduced the

21 New road through a barren landscape

20 Homelands of the main ethnic groups

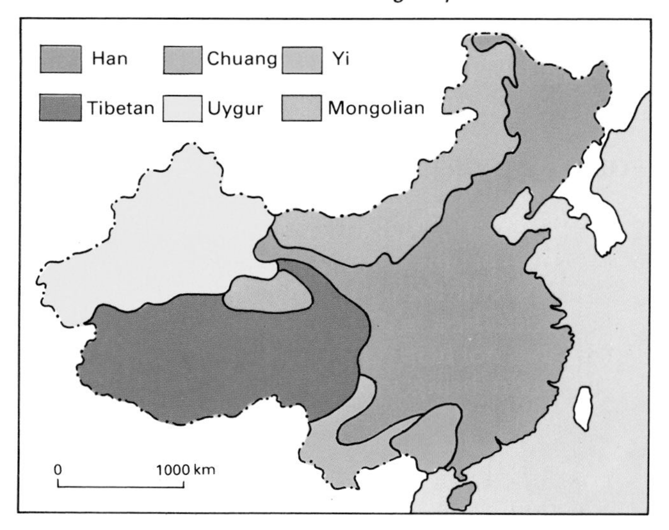

22 Sheep herding in Tibet

23 *Settled life in the valleys*

development schemes in Tibet and returned some freedom to the Tibetans. The Tibetan language is being encouraged and monasteries and temples restored (24). Tibetans want to be independent but believe the Chinese are only trying to restore tradition to help the tourist trade.

24 *Temples are being restored*

25 *Animal rearing in Inner Mongolia*

The Mongolians

Two million Mongolians live on the grasslands of Inner Mongolia, in north China. They speak their own language and are Tibetan Buddhists. Their life is hard because of cold winters, strong winds and little rainfall. The Mongolians raise sheep, goats, cattle, horses and camels (25). The grass is poor and they move with their animals to find pasture.

Since 1958, the government has set up state farms for wheat and maize cultivation and opened iron ore mines, developed roads and settled Chinese there. The Mongolians are encouraged to live a more settled life. Stone walls are built to shelter crops and animals, and wells dug to provide water supplies. These Mongolians have built houses, and use their yurts for storage. The Chinese have better control over a settled population.

FOLLOW-UP WORK

1 What are the main differences between life in the outer regions and east China?
2 Why have the Chinese built roads to the outer regions?
3 Why do the Chinese want the Tibetans and Mongolians to live a settled life?
4 Why are the Tibetans hostile to the Chinese?
5 'The outer regions are a buffer between China proper and surrounding countries such as India and the USSR.' What does this mean?

Developing the country's resources

China has huge supplies of coal and minerals but there are many problems bringing these into production. These are the main problems.

- Resources are often located in hostile environments such as mountains and deserts.
- Resources are often remote from factories in cities in the south and east of China.
- Most mineral ores including iron, tin and aluminium, are low grade and poor quality.
- China's main resource is labour and there is a shortage of capital (money) and modern technology. Some coal mines, for example, are modern (26) but 50 000 others are pick-and-shovel operations.
- Road and rail transport is inadequate to get resources, such as coal, to widely spread markets. Canal transport is still important (27).
- West-to-east-flowing rivers hinder north-to-south transport.
- There are inadequate supplies of electricity to refine the low-quality ores.

26 A modern coal mine

27 Ancient canals for a modern economy

28 Resources location map

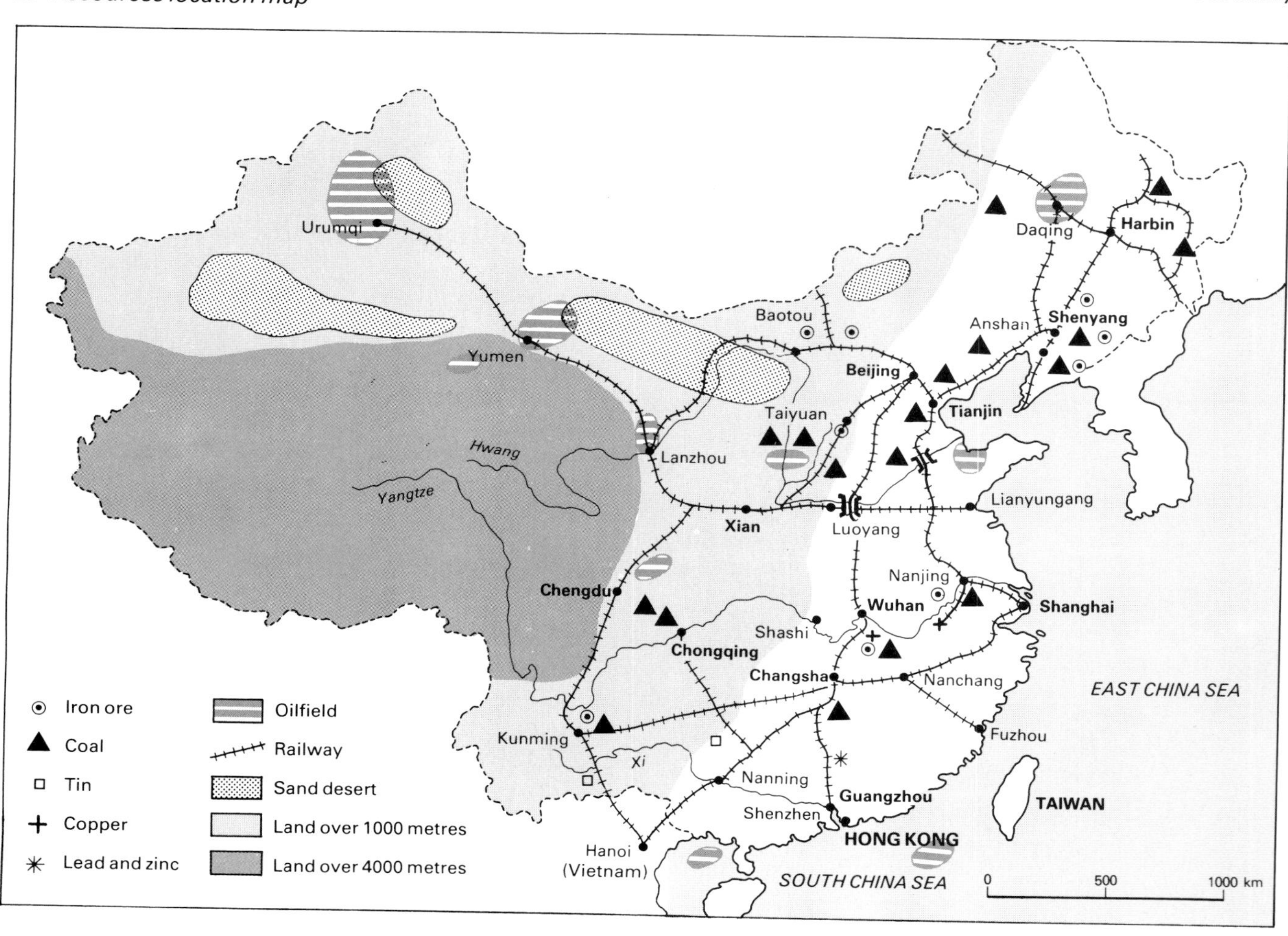

29 *Bridge across the Yangtze at Nanjing*

Since the 1950s, the Communist government has developed the road and rail network (28) with bridges (29) and dams across the rivers, and made big increases in the output of coal, oil, iron ore (30) and other minerals. The aim has been to supply growing industries and reduce the need for imports. The pie graph (31) shows the pattern of consumption of primary energy.

30 *Growth in production, 1949–86*

Product	Coal	Oil	Iron ore
	(output in million tonnes)		
1949	32	0.1	4
1959	300	4	100
1969	258	20	72
1979	635	106	110
1986	870	131	130

32 *Building a dam on the Yangtze*

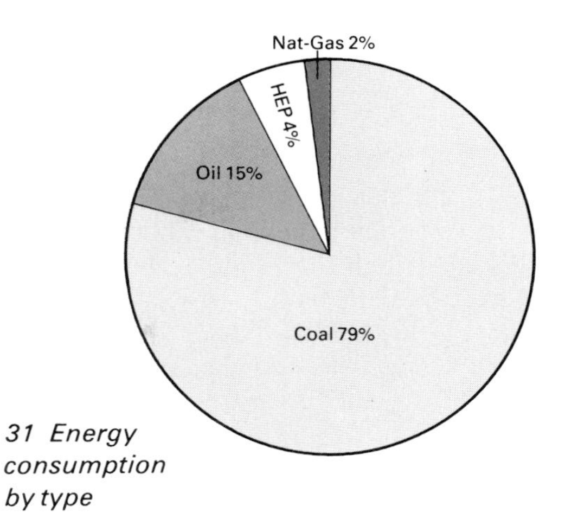

31 *Energy consumption by type*

> *PIE GRAPH*
>
> A circle which is divided into sectors. Each sector is proportional in size to the value it represents. In this example, 1% = 3.6° of the circle.
> Compare the pie graph for China's energy consumption pattern with those of other countries. Ask for the worksheet.

FOLLOW-UP WORK

1 Use map (28) for this exercise.
 (a) What problems will there be for developing mineral resources at Urumqi?
 (b) How far is the rail journey for carrying coal from the mines near Taiyuan to Guangzhou (Canton)?

2 Suggest reasons why industries in south China buy coal and iron ore from Australia.

3 (a) Suggest reasons for building dams (32) on the Yangtze.
 (b) Suggest a city location on map (28) which would be a good site for a dam.

4 Study the pie graph (31).
 (a) What is China's main source of energy?
 (b) Why does China depend so much on this energy resource?

5 Offshore explorations by Western oil companies have found only small amounts of oil and gas.
 (a) Why does China need Western companies, from Europe and the USA, to find oil?
 (b) Why is China improving production methods in existing onshore oilfields?
 (c) If no more oil is found, how will this affect China's industrial growth in the future?

Industry: three systems in one country

When the Communists came to power in 1949 they decided to develop basic industries. There were already large steelworks in Anshan and other cities in north-east China which the Japanese built when they occupied this part of China between 1931 and 1945. Table (33) shows how steel output has increased since then. Most steelworks use local raw materials but the Baoshan steelworks, which opened in Shanghai in 1985, uses high-grade iron ore from Australia, Brazil and India. The steel is needed to make machinery, railway lines, farm equipment, bicycles, households goods and a host of other products.

33 Industrial output, 1949–86

Year	*Steel (million tonnes)*	*Cotton cloth (million metres)*	*Bicycles (millions)*	*TV sets (millions)*
1949	0.2	1 900	0.1	–
1965	18.0	6 280	1.8	0.04
1979	35.0	12 150	10.0	1.30
1986	52.0	15 800	36.0	17.00

34 Oil refinery near Beijing

35 Old technology in the steelworks

BASIC INDUSTRY

An industry which provides the materials for other industries. The steel industry supports many manufacturing industries such as construction, machinery and household goods.

When oil was discovered, oil refineries were built (34). There is a large output of chemical fertilizers, synthetic fibres and plastics. The long-established textile industry has also been expanded using local resources and supplying more than a billion people with clothing (33).

China's large factories have many features in common:

- They are owned by the state.
- They are run by managers, committees and work teams.
- Material inputs are controlled by the state, which decides the suppliers.
- There is a high input of labour. The Baotou steelworks, for example, employs 60 000 workers to make less than 2 million tonnes of steel a year.
- Processes involve old technology such as open-hearth furnaces in steelworks (35).
- Output is often low and poor quality and is bought by the state at fixed prices.

36 *Light industry in a small town*

- Wages are fixed by the state with no incentives to raise output.
- Jobs are secure and workers live near to the factory which often provides houses, shops, schools, clinics and a cinema.

In recent years the factories have been given more freedom to run their own operations, compete for supplies and markets and make bonus payments to workers for increased output.

There is a different system in the countryside. When communes were set up, each one had factories to make farm equipment, waterpumps, fertilizers, bricks, cement, furniture, food and clothing. Since 1980, these enterprises have been leased out to individuals and to groups of people who have pooled their money and formed a co-operative. They can hire and sack people, choose their own suppliers and freely market their products for a good profit. This money can be invested in new equipment. New industries are being set up (36) to meet the needs of people who now have money to spend. They are light industries. These industries are providing thousands of jobs in rural areas which stops people drifting into cities to find work. This is

> *LIGHT INDUSTRY*
>
> The manufacture of goods which are light, small in size and easy to transport.

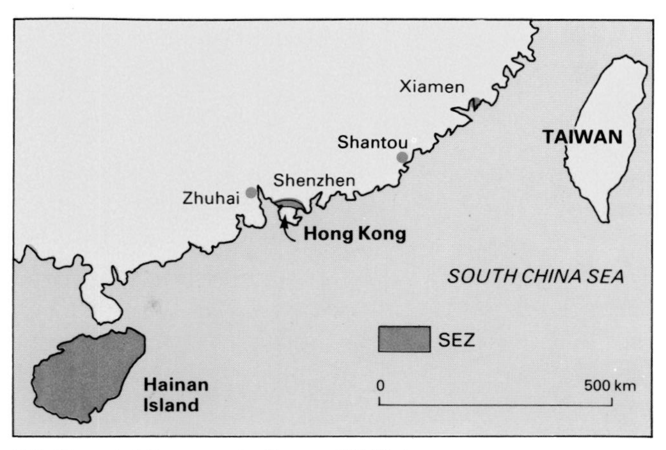

37 *Special Economic Zones (SEZs)*

different from most other developing countries where factories are usually in just a few cities.

The Chinese have seen neighbours Hong Kong, Taiwan and South Korea develop modern export industries. This is because advanced industrial countries such as Japan and the USA have built factories there. The advanced country builds the factory, installs modern assembly-line equipment, supplies the components and takes advantage of the developing country's cheap labour, cheap land and low taxes. The products, such as mass-produced plastic toys, video tape recorders and electric household goods, can be sold on world markets at a lower price than other countries can make them.

China has become part of this system with new foreign-owned factories in five Special Economic Zones (SEZs) shown on map (37). Shenzhen (38) looks more like neighbouring Hong Kong than any city in China. This is China's 'open door' policy. The country will soon learn the new technology, build more factories and become one of the world's most important industrial countries.

38 *Shenzhen*

39 Bicycles and buses in the city

FOLLOW-UP WORK

1 Why did the Communist government start industrial development with basic industries such as steelmaking?
2 What advantages does China have for each of these industries:
 (a) steel,
 (b) bicycles (39),
 (c) cotton cloth?
3 Suggest reasons for these locations:
 (a) large steelworks on the coast at Shanghai,
 (b) SEZs on the coast in the south of China.
4 (a) What is the difference in labour and output between the Baotou steelworks in China and the Oita steelworks in Japan? (Look back to page 51.)
 (b) Why is there such a big difference between the two steelworks?
5 Why is China allowing
 (a) more freedom in the running of her big factories,
 (b) foreign companies to build factories there?
6 'Japan is the industrial core and China is in the periphery.' What does this mean? (Consult page 57 to help you.)
7 Why is it an advantage for China to set up factories in the countryside where 80 per cent of the population live, rather than locate all the factories in cities, which happens in most other developing countries?

Tourism: a new industry

The Chinese are tied to the land and to the factory in the city. They neither have the money nor the time to visit different parts of the country except perhaps to visit relatives. Until 1976, China was also closed to visitors from other countries except for a few guests invited by the Communist government.

The new 'open door' policy has made it possible for people to visit China, mainly in organised groups. There were more than 20 million tourists in 1987 and they came mainly from Japan, Hong Kong, USA and countries in Europe. The state runs a string of about 700 tourist hotels located in the main places of interest. There is also an internal tourist air service with other travel by rail, road and river. A typical tour from Britain is shown on map (40), with details above it. It costs about £2000.

> *TOURISM*
>
> Organised journeys through a country from one place to another for pleasure. The tourist industry provides accommodation, transport, guides, souvenir shops and other services for the visitor.

FOLLOW-UP WORK

1 (a) Mark the tour of China onto your own copy of map (40). How many kilometres will the tourist travel on this tour in China?
 (b) Explain the route chosen.
 (c) Why is so much travel packed into one tour?
 (d) List each visit under one or more of these headings: CULTURAL/SOCIAL/SCENIC. What conclusions do you draw about the type of holiday this is?
 (e) What would you like and dislike about this type of holiday?
 (f) What types of transport are used? Say why.
 (g) How will cost affect travel from Britain?
2 (a) Why will individual travel be difficult?
 (b) Why might individual travel provide a better idea of normal daily life?
3 Suggest reasons why few Chinese but large numbers of Japanese are tourists.
4 Study the advantages and problems of tourism (43).
 (a) Do the advantages outweigh the problems? Add your comments.
 (b) Which is the worst problem? Can you suggest a solution?

Tour of China

1. Departure from Heathrow Airport. Flight to Beijing.
2. Beijing, capital of China. Visits to The Great Wall (41) built by the first emperor in the third century BC, The Forbidden City (42), first built in the fifteenth century by a Ming emperor, the Temple of Heaven and the Summer Palace. 3 days.
3. Flight to Xian, the ancient capital of China. View the 6000 life-sized terracotta warriors. These pottery soldiers guard the entrance to the tomb of the first emperor and date back to the third century. 2 days.
4. Flight to Chongqing, an industrial city on the Yangtze River. You can stroll along the river banks, view terraced fields and see crowded street markets. Urban and rural life intermingle. 1 day.
5. Sail along the Yangtze River through its great gorges to Yueyang. 2 days.
6. Overnight train to Shanghai. Great port and industrial city. Contrast the Western-style colonial buildings from nineteenth-century European occupation with the colourful Chinese street life. Visit the Jade Buddha Temple. 3 days.
7. Day-trip by bus from Shanghai to Suzhou. See traditional life and crafts including silk weaving and embroidery. 1 day.

40 Tourist route map

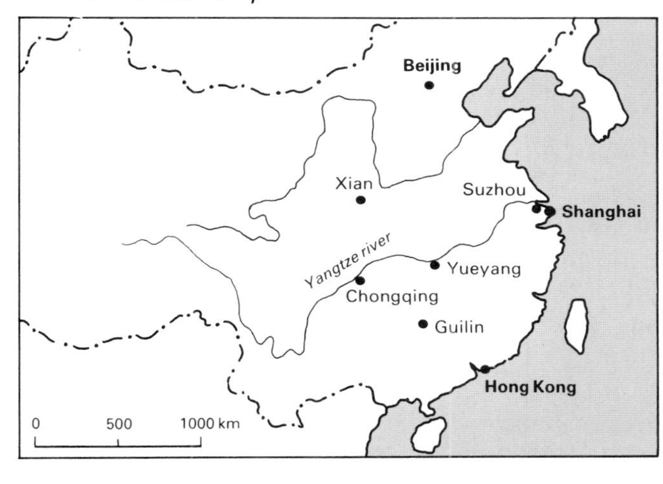

41 The Great Wall

42 The Forbidden City

8. Flight to Guilin from Shanghai. See the pinnacles of weathered limestone which have inspired Chinese artists for centuries. Sail along the Li River to view the green countryside with paddyfields and water buffalo. 2 days.
9. Flight to Hong Kong. See the towering office blocks and flats, busy harbour, shops and exciting night life. 2 days.
10. Return flight to London.

43 The advantages and problems of tourism

Advantages

1. Tourists can gain a better understanding of a different culture and way of life. They will be uplifted by seeing magnificent buildings and scenery.
2. The tourist industry earns foreign currency which can be used to import materials and technology needed for the modernisation of the country.
3. Tourism provides jobs in hotels, transport, souvenir crafts and other services.
4. Developments for tourists such as air communications can benefit local people.

Problems

1. Guided tours may give a false impression of the normal way of life. Special privileges for tourists in shops, museums and accommodation, plus the intrusion of cameras, might upset Chinese people.
2. The Chinese are made more aware of their own poor standard of living when compared with the wealth exhibited by tourists.
3. Large numbers of tourists at a few popular places could damage the environment.
4. The expense of building hotels and providing new air routes reduces the earnings from tourism.

Cities

There have been cities in China for thousands of years. Farmers began to grow crops more than 3000 years ago. They grew more food than they needed themselves. Craftsmen gathered together in cities and exchanged their goods for the farmers' surplus food. The process of urbanisation has continued since then. By the year 1100, five cities had over 1 million people.

When the Communists came to power in 1949, 10 per cent of the population lived in cities, nine of which had a million people. When heavy industries were built in the 1950s, more people migrated to the cities to find jobs. The urban population doubled in ten years and the youthful population brought a large natural increase in the following years. By 1987, 21 per cent of China's 1 billion people lived in towns and cities. There were twenty-one cities with more than 1 million people (44). As in most other developing countries, rapid urban growth has resulted in problems of overcrowding and

44 Cities with a million people

46 Blocks of flats in every city

45 Solving city problems

1. Forced movement of millions of school leavers and unemployed people out of the cities into the communes (as happened in the 1960s).
2. Stop the movement of people into the city, except people with skills needed in the new modern factories. City dwellers to be registered in order to get housing, jobs and food rations.
3. The one-child family policy to be strictly applied in the city.
4. New small industrial enterprises encouraged in every village and small town to keep all the surplus rural labour in the countryside.
5. New blocks of flats built on the edge of every city (46).
6. Private enterprises encouraged in the city to create jobs repairing clothes (47) and televisions, and in shops and restaurants, for example.

Which solutions would you favour and which would you be against? Say why.
Why can many of these methods be carried out in China but not in many other developing countries in the world?

47 Tailoring provides jobs

48 *Beijing street scene*

unemployment. Table (45) shows some of the methods which have been used to tackle these problems.

Living in Beijing

Beijing (Peking) is the capital city and centre of culture, administration, commerce and industry. In 1949, the population was 1.6 million, most of whom lived in poverty in crowded housing. In 1988, the population was 5.9 million. Wide roads and blocks of flats have replaced narrow alleys and shanty dwellings (48).

The Chang family rent one room in a nine-storey block (49). They share a toilet and kitchen with two other families. Mrs Chang works in a state-owned shop and Mr Chang works in a local steelworks. They work eight hours a day, for six days a week. They have a few days' holiday each year. Their wages cover the cost of food and clothing with a little to buy a radio, television, sewing machine and books.

Mr Chang cycles to work. There are 4 million bicycles in Beijing, so there is a great deal of noise and congestion when he goes to work on the new cycle lanes.

The youngest daughter goes to primary school. The eldest daughter is in a class of forty-five in secondary school. She studies full time for six days a week. On the syllabus are languages, science and politics. Mr Chang is a member of the committee which runs the neighbourhood. He helps to organise the schools, clinic, law and order and social events.

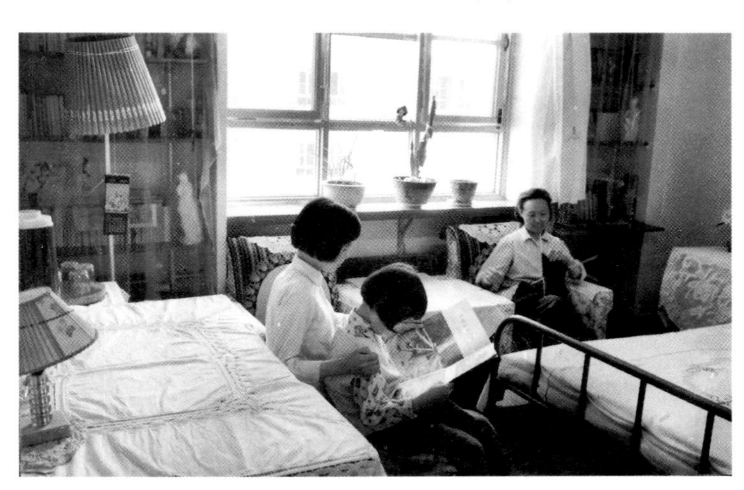

49 *Inside a Beijing flat*

FOLLOW-UP WORK

1 What improvements have been made in housing in Beijing since 1949?
2 Draw a sketch of photograph (49). Label the furniture in this typical one-roomed, state-owned flat. Add a few sentences comparing this with your home.
3 What might be the advantages of having a neighbourhood committee?
4 Make a list of the clues which tell you that photograph (48) was not taken in Britain.
5 Beijing has trebled its population since 1949. What problems might this have brought for (a) housing and jobs, (b) schools and hospitals, (c) roads and traffic, (d) coping with waste products?

Hong Kong

Crowded city-state

Hong Kong is a British colony on the south coast of China (1) and it is one of the most crowded places on Earth. In the nineteenth century, when China was politically weak and Britain was a strong trading nation seeking markets and power in the Far East, Hong Kong Island (1842), the Kowloon peninsula (1860) and the New Territories (1898) came into British hands (1). This gave Britain the best harbour on the south coast of China from which to trade with China and surrounding countries (2). Hong Kong has been a trading nation since that time. The final agreement was a ninety-nine-year lease from China, which means that Hong Kong returns to Chinese sovereignty in 1997.

When Britain took control of Hong Kong there were 12 000 people living there. They were farmers and fishermen living on what was mainly a barren and hilly 1000 square kilometres of land. Since then, the population has grown to more than 5 million (3), with some areas packed with over 100 000 people per square kilometre.

Ninety-eight per cent of the population are Chinese who have come from surrounding parts of China and they share the same traditions, culture and Cantonese language.

2 *Victoria Harbour*

1 *Hong Kong: the state and surrounding countries*

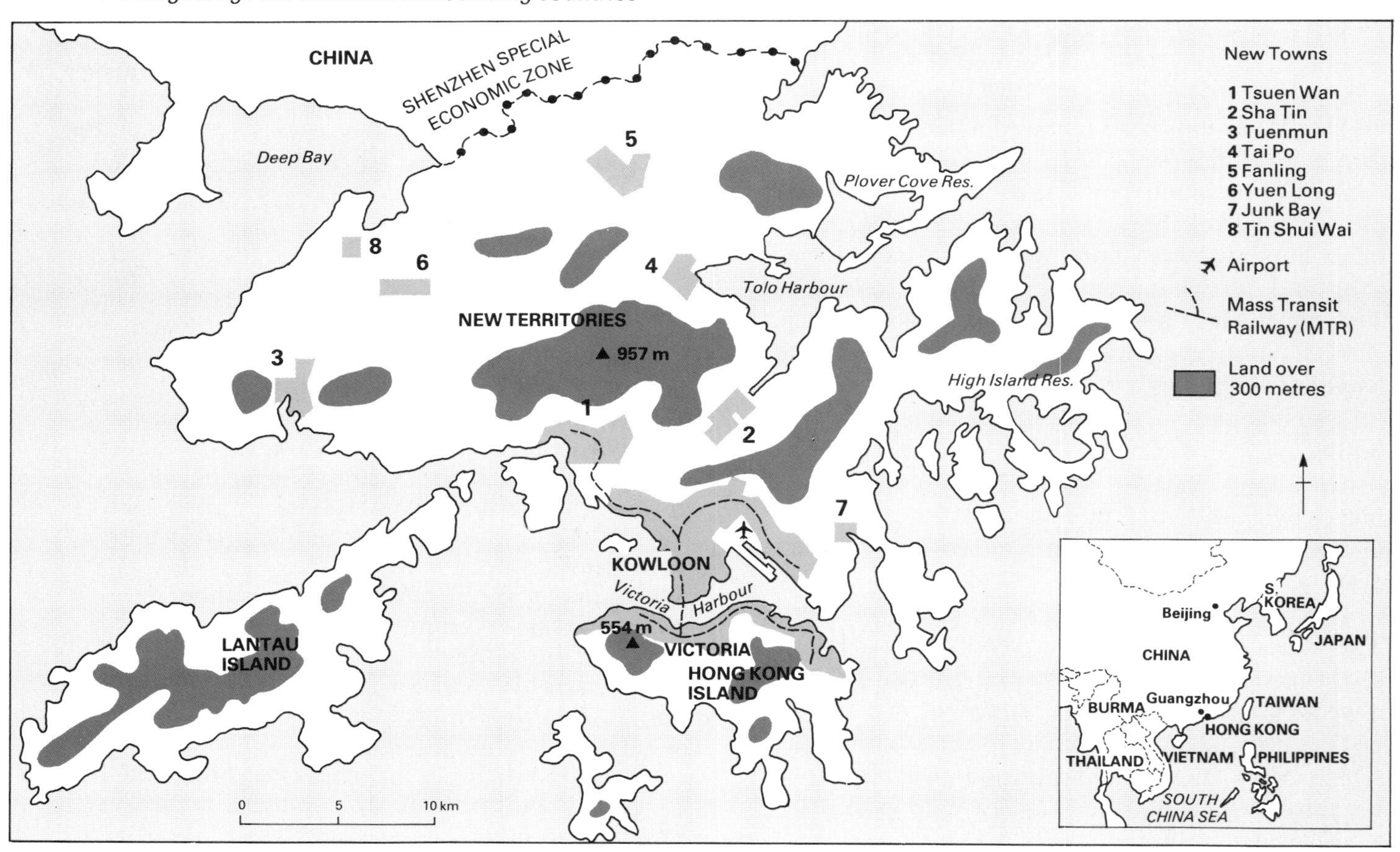

3 Growth of Hong Kong, 1911–87

Year	Million people
1911	0.5
1921	0.6
1931	0.8
1941	1.0
1951	2.3
1961	3.1
1971	3.9
1981	5.0
1987	5.6

The main influx of people came when civil war brought the Communists to power in 1949. Landowners, businessmen and their families, for example, fled for their lives to Hong Kong. Even though there is tight security along the border with China, more immigrants find their way to Hong Kong every year. They will find a home with relatives or friends or build a shack in a squatter settlement. Out of every five people who try to reach Hong Kong in this way, three are caught by Chinese border guards, one by Hong Kong patrols and one reaches base in Hong Kong.

Added to these are Vietnamese 'boat people' (4), who make a three-week journey across the South China Sea to reach Hong Kong (1). In 1975, at the end of the Vietnam War, most arrivals were refugees from a Communist-controlled country. Recent arrivals (5) are poor farmers and fishermen who arrive in hope of a better life in Hong Kong or a chance of being re-settled in the USA, Europe or Australia.

Fifty-nine per cent of the present population was born in Hong Kong, 37 per cent in China and 4 per cent in other countries. It is a youthful population and the birth rate far outstrips the death rate (6) which results in a large natural increase every year. The infant mortality rate continues to fall as child health care improves each year.

4 Boat people arrive in Hong Kong as refugees

5 More immigrants arrive seeking a better life

6 Birth and death rates

Year	Birth rate (per 1000 population)	Death rate (per 1000 population)	Infant mortality rate (per 1000 live births)
1976	17.4	5.0	13.7
1981	16.8	4.8	9.7
1986	13.0	4.7	7.5

FOLLOW-UP WORK

1 Measure the distances from north to south and from east to west across Hong Kong, using map (1), and across the Isle of Wight using an atlas. How do the measurements compare?

2 Draw a line graph to show population growth between 1911 and 1987. Use a scale of 1 million people to 2 cm. What two factors caused the growth of population shown on the graph?

3 What was the average density of population per square kilometre in (a) 1941, and (b) 1981?

4 Photograph (2) was taken from Victoria Peak (554 metres) on Hong Kong Island. Find this on map (1).
   (a) In which direction was the camera pointing?
   (b) Name the city top right and the new town top left.
   (c) What evidence is there on the photograph and map to explain why settlement is more dense along the coast than inland?

A newly industrialised country

Hong Kong has always depended on trade. The fine sheltered harbour (2) at the gateway to China and within easy reach of many countries in Asia and America, around the rim of the Pacific Ocean, has made Hong Kong one of the busiest ports in the world. Entrepot trade has always been important. Goods flow into Hong Kong from surrounding countries and are re-distributed to world markets.

It was a natural development from this trade that Hong Kong should begin to process and manufacture raw materials before exporting them for a good profit. This early stage in industrialisation came in the 1950s. China's new Communist government stopped trading with the world, so Hong Kong had to find other ways to survive. The answer came with the refugees from China. Many had owned textile factories in Canton and Shanghai and they brought money, machines and manufacturing skills to Hong Kong. Cotton textiles and clothing are still the most important industries in Hong Kong (7, 8).

Hong Kong has mainly labour-intensive light industries which can operate in small rooms of multi-storey blocks (9). This is because Hong Kong lacks space but has plenty of labour. Plastic flowers, utensils and toys, watches (10) and clocks and electronic goods are made from materials and parts imported from other countries (11). Most of the goods are exported to the USA, China, and countries in Europe (12). As you can see, trade remains the basis of Hong Kong's economy.

8 Hong Kong factories, 1986

Products	*Number of factories (thousands)*	*Number of workers (thousands)*
Clothing	9	264
Textiles	5	116
Electrical goods	2	115
Plastic products	5	89
Metal goods	7	64
Printing/paper	5	47
Scientific equipment, watches and clocks	2	40
Others	13	129
Total	48	864

ENTREPÔT

A place which collects goods from surrounding countries, stores them, and sends them to other countries when they are wanted.

7 Cotton textiles are dyed and dried

9 Plastic products made in a small workshop

10 *Watchmaking: all young women*

11 *Imports, 1986*

Items	*% of total*
Raw materials and parts	43
(of which textile yarns and fabrics	15)
Consumer goods	31
Capital goods, including machinery	14
Food	9
Fuel	3

Main suppliers: China 30%, Japan 20%, Taiwan 9%, USA 8%, UK 3%

12 *Exports, 1986*

Items	*% of total*
Clothing	34
Electronics	22
Plastic products	8
Watches and clocks	8
Textiles	7
Electrical household goods	3
Metal products	3
Others	15

Main markets: USA 42%, China 12%, West Germany 7%, UK 6%, Japan 4%

FOLLOW-UP WORK

1 Answer TRUE or FALSE to each of these statements.
   A Hong Kong buys most of its raw materials and parts from other countries.
   B As a British colony, Hong Kong depends on Britain for trade.
   C Hong Kong buys most of its products from countries around the Pacific Ocean.
   D Hong Kong makes most of the machinery it needs for its industries.
   E The average factory has fewer than twenty workers.
   F Young women are often employed because they have nimble fingers and work for low wages.
   G Hong Kong depends heavily on the USA to sell its products.
   H Hong Kong has a favourable balance of trade with Japan.
2 Give reasons why light industries are most important in Hong Kong.
3 'Hong Kong exports to live but lives on imports.' What does this mean?
4 An American computer company in San Francisco (Silicon Valley) plans to assemble integrated circuits into silicon chips in Hong Kong. These will be flown back to the USA for testing and used in a new computer to be sold in America.
   (a) Which of the factors shown in figure (13) will have attracted the company to Hong Kong?
   (b) Suggest why all the research, testing and final assembly is done in the USA and not in Hong Kong.

13 *Factors helping the growth of industry*

1 A busy port with modern container terminal
2 Major international airport
3 Free enterprise. People aim to make a profit from small enterprises
4 Cheap and plentiful labour
5 Low taxes
6 Products are made for export in competition with other countries such as Taiwan
7 Profits are put back into new machinery
8 Workers are becoming skilled in many manufacturing and assembly processes
9 A flexible labour force able to transfer skills from one industry to another
10 Hundreds of multinational companies from the USA are already operating in Hong Kong. Most profit can be returned to the home country

A problem of people

Hong Kong is a very small country. Over 5 million people are crowded onto 1000 square kilometres of land, most of which is too steep for settlement.

FOLLOW-UP WORK

Study the problems that are numbered 1 to 7. Some ways of helping to solve these problems are shown on page 89. These are not placed in the correct order.

1 Match each plan to a problem.
2 Write a few lines about each problem. Say whether the plan will solve, ease or have no effect on the problem.

Problem 1: immigrants

In 1979, 108 000 Chinese immigrants came illegally into Hong Kong. Most of them settled into a home and found a job, and were allowed to stay. In the same year, 70 000 Chinese were legally allowed into Hong Kong to join their families.

15 Kowloon street

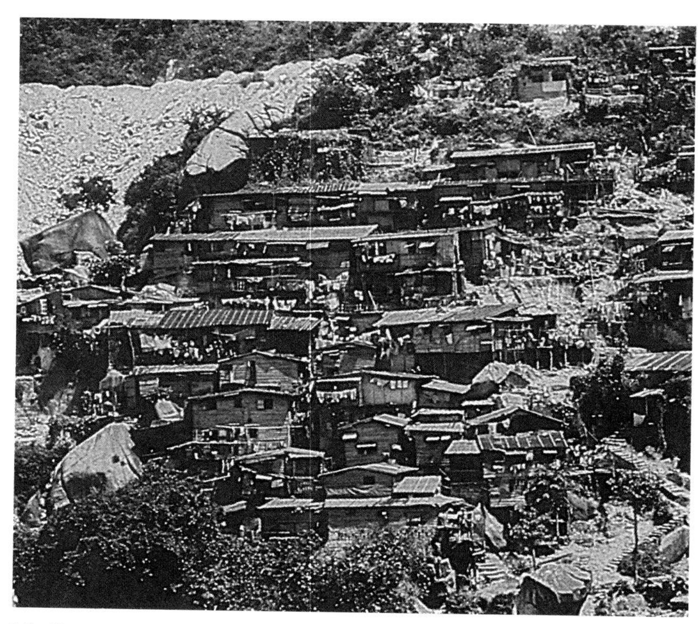

14 Squatter shacks

Problem 2: squatter areas

Immigrants who cannot find homes live in shanty towns (14). Squatter shacks are made from packing-case wood and corrugated iron. In 1988, 100 000 families lived in squatter areas.

Problem 3: working conditions

Most people work long hours for low wages. Children are often sent to work instead of going to school.

Problem 4: overcrowded streets

The streets of Kowloon (15) and Victoria are congested with people and traffic. The ferries between the two cities are overcrowded.

Problem 5: food supplies

Most of Hong Kong is steep, infertile hillside. Only 9 per cent of the land can be cultivated. The country cannot grow enough food for the large population.

Problem 6: water supplies

There are no natural lakes or large rivers. Hong Kong depends on China to supply drinking water.

Problem 7: drugs and crime

This area of the world has a history of drug trading. Supplies of heroin come mainly from Thailand. There are 80 000 drug addicts in Hong Kong. The crime rate is high because of drug taking, poverty, overcrowding and hard working conditions. In 1986, 81 000 crimes were reported. Half of them were solved.

Plan A: mass transit railway

The railway (16) shown on map (1) opened in 1980. It has been extended to 39 kilometres passing through Victoria, Kowloon, and Tsuen Wan. It carries 1.6 million people each weekday.

Plan B: compulsory school

Education up to the age of 15 was made compulsory in 1980. Young people aged 15 to 17 are only allowed to work eight hours a day for six days a week.

Plan C: dams and lakes

Inlets of the sea are dammed. Sea water is drained out and freshwater reservoirs are made. Plover Cove reservoir was made in 1967 and High Island reservoir in 1979 (1).

Plan D: duck and fish ponds

Farmers are using the land intensively. Rice growing has been replaced by vegetable, pig, poultry and fish farming (17).

Plan E: new towns

Over 35 000 new low-cost flats are built each year. Eight new towns (1) housed 2.5 million people in 1988. Each new town has blocks of flats (18), factories, offices, schools, clinics, play areas and police stations. Squatter areas are not upgraded but are knocked down when new flats are built.

Plan F: police stations

The Royal Hong Kong Police Force has 26 000 men. This number will be increased. Police stations will be built in every district. Over 700 police officers are used to stop illegal immigration. There is a drugs squad.

16 Train at Kowloon

Plan G: border patrols

In 1980, laws were passed to allow the arrest, and return to China, of any person who has entered Hong Kong illegally. Everyone over 15 years of age must carry an identity card. It is illegal to employ a person without an identity card. Army and Navy border patrols are to be increased. Many Vietnamese boat people have been returned home since 1988.

17 Duck and fish ponds

18 New town housing

Singapore

1 *Office blocks and old buildings*

Singapore is one of the busiest ports and business cities in the world. Photograph (1) shows both old and new Singapore. The fifty-two-storey office block belongs to the Oversea-Chinese Banking Corporation. It overlooks the Singapore River, crowded with sampans, and towers over the old shophouses. Singapore has grown into a modern city-state from a small forested island in the nineteenth century.

Britain's early trade with China was organised by the British East India Company. Ships set sail for China loaded with opium and cotton cloth from Calcutta in India. China tea was the main cargo on the ships returning from Canton to India. Sailing ships needed a stopping place to take on water and supplies. The island of Singapore was chosen for this purpose in 1819. It has a deep, sheltered harbour located halfway between India and China.

Singapore soon became a busy port. Workers needed at the port were coolies from China and convicts brought from India.

The port became busier when the Suez Canal was opened in 1869, and steamships replaced sailing ships on the routes to the Far East.

Singapore's position, at the heart of South-east Asia, made her a perfect entrepôt. Boats loaded with coffee, rice, spices, tin and gold came to the new port of Singapore from Java and Sumatra. Return cargoes for the islands, including iron, opium and cloth, came from Britain, India and China.

ENTREPÔT: TRADE GAME

Each player owns a trading company with warehouses in Singapore. As you play the game the nature of entrepôt trade and the importance of Singapore's location for supplying world markets are revealed. Ask for details.

Modern developments on a crowded island

Since 1960, Singapore has become a newly industrialised country. Many features of the country and its development are shown in chart (2) and on map (3).

A City-state: Singapore comprises one large island and fifty-seven islets with a total 622 square kilometres.
B Population: 2.6 million people (1987) live in Singapore. They are mainly Chinese (76 per cent), Malays (15 per cent) and Indians (6 per cent).
C British colonial development: the deep harbour and strategic location on world trade routes favoured entrepôt trade, which remains important.
D Land use: half the land is built upon. Only 6 per cent is farmed, with intensive vegetable growing, pigs and poultry. Only small areas of rainforest and swampforest remain.
E Mainland state: Singapore relies on Malaysia for large amounts of trade and for supplies of drinking water.
F Imports: local resources are limited and Singapore depends on imports of food, raw materials and manufactures. Japan (20 per cent), USA (15 per cent) and Malaysia (13 per cent) are the main suppliers.
G Oil: Singapore has the world's third largest oil refining industry after Houston and Rotterdam. Imports are from the Pacific region and the Middle East.
H Industry: this was labour-intensive in the 1960s (clothing) using cheap labour and entrepôt trade. Since the 1970s more capital- and technology-intensive industries (electronics) have been set up with multinationals from the USA and Japan, government help, and a more skilled labour force.
I Exports: the main markets are the USA (23 per cent), Malaysia (16 per cent) and Japan (9 per cent).
J Business: the time-zone location helps business transactions in Asia.
K Transport: there is a busy international airport, a Mass Rapid Transport (MRT) railway developed in the 1980s to carry 600 000 people each day on a 66-kilometre network, and a new road Expressways network.
L Housing: the government's housing programme has built new blocks of flats in Singapore City and in residential estates in all parts of the island, housing 85 per cent of the population (4).

2 Singapore: features and development

3 Singapore: the state and surrounding countries

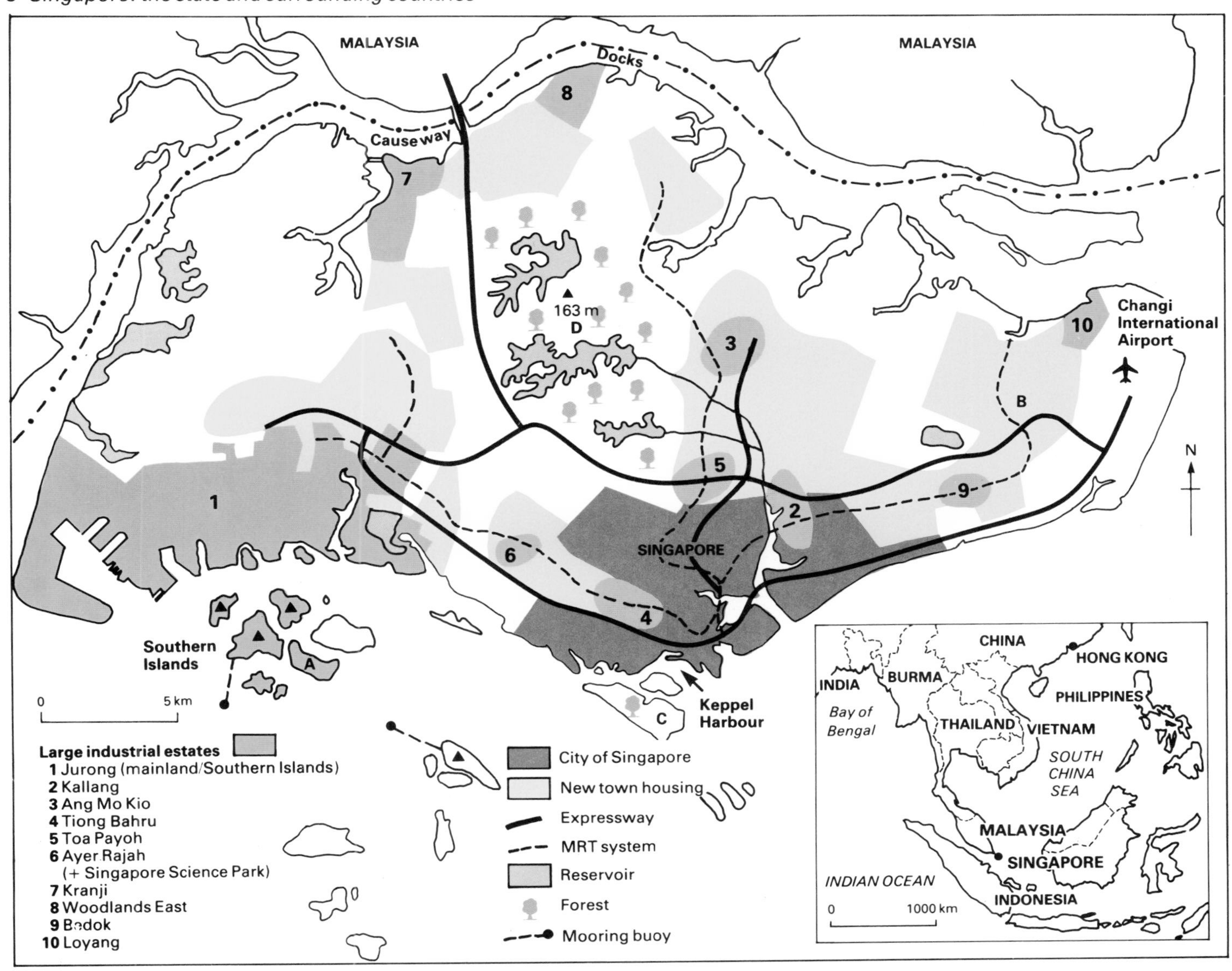

4 *New blocks of flats*

FOLLOW-UP WORK

1 Suggest reasons for building
   (a) large blocks of flats,
   (b) housing estates in many parts of the island,
   (c) a Mass Rapid Transport system,
   (d) an expressway to Malaysia.
2 Study the features A to L in chart (2).
   (a) Which are similar and which are different in Hong Kong (see pages 84 to 89)?
   (b) Which features have helped the industrial growth of Singapore?
3 (a) Why is there more trade with the USA than with Hong Kong?
   (b) The USA increased taxes on goods entering the USA from Singapore and Hong Kong in 1989. Suggest why this was done and what effect it might have on Singapore.
4 Study map (3). Suggest reasons for locating each of these developments:
   (a) an oil refinery at site A,
   (b) a new industrial estate at site B,
   (c) a holiday resort at site C,
   (d) a nature reserve at site D.

5 *Jurong industrial estate*

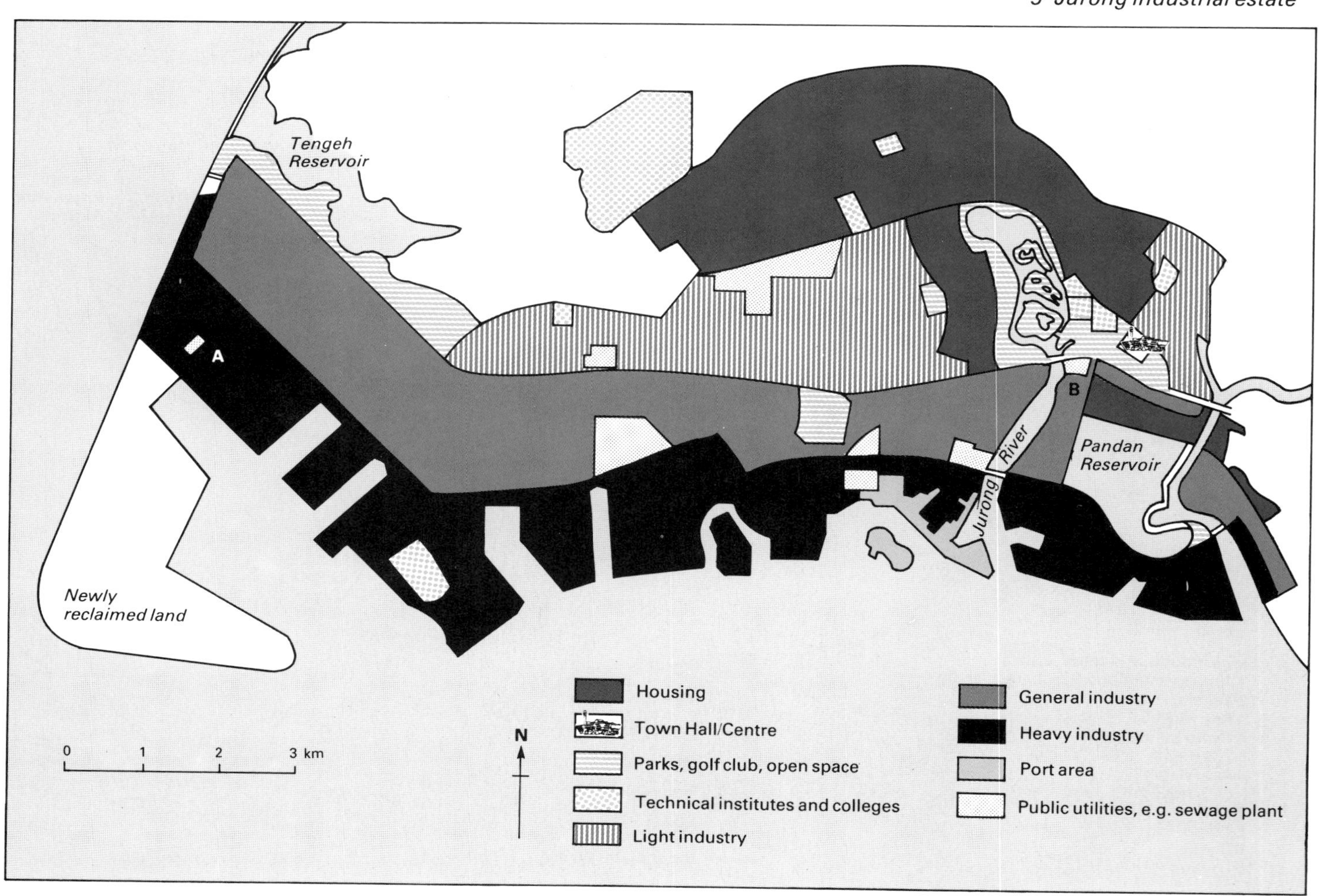

Industrial estates

Seventy per cent of all the factories in Singapore are on modern industrial estates. There are twenty-four estates located in all parts of the country. Ten of these are shown on map (3). More than half of the factories are owned by multinational companies with headquarters in the USA, Japan, Britain and West Germany.

Some estates are in the middle of densely settled housing areas. These have flatted factories which are blocks with a large number of light industries which do not cause too much noise or pollution. The largest estates have been carefully planned as self-contained centres with factories, offices, housing, schools, clinics, child-care centres, shops, entertainments and parks.

The first and the largest estate is Jurong Town in the west of the island (3, 5). In 1960 this was an almost empty area of swamp, forest and prawn ponds. Work began in 1961 to level the hills, fill the swamps, reclaim land from the sea, and build roads and factories. Heavy industries were sited along the coast (6) with light industries further inland. At the same time as this development was taking place, oil refineries were built on the Southern Islands. In 1988 Jurong had a population of 232 000 with 99 000 people employed in 1935 factories (7).

The Jurong Town Corporation, which was formed in 1968 to run the estate, was given the job of setting up all the other estates in Singapore. The aim is to make the estates as attractive as possible to companies wanting to start production in a newly industrialised country (8).

7 Standard factory units in Jurong

8 Attractions of the industrial estate

- Roads, sewers, drains, water and electricity supplies and telecommunications are provided.
- The land is made level and ready for any company that wants to build its own factory.
- Ready-built, single-storey, small and medium-sized standard factories are available for any company wanting to start up operations right away (7).
- Technical Institutes are available to send workers to in order to increase their technical knowledge and skills.
- Warehouses and port facilities are available.

6 View across eastern Jurong

FOLLOW-UP WORK

Study maps (3) and (5) and the photographs (6) and (7) of the Jurong industrial estate, which has been planned with zones for housing and different types of industry. Attempt the questions based upon them.

Industry

1 What type of factories will have been built in Tiong Bahru industrial estate numbered 4 on map (3)? Explain your answer.
2 Find, on map (5), the area shown in photograph (6).
  (a) In which direction was the camera pointing?
  (b) Name the river and reservoir.
  (c) What advantages does the area have for heavy industries?
3 Study photograph (7) which shows a light industrial area in Jurong (map 5).
  (a) In which direction was the camera pointing? Say how you came to your answer.
  (b) Why would an electronics company find this a good place to start up operations?
  (c) What advantages will there be in having many factories, such as these, close to each other? (See page 64.)

Housing

1 Study maps (3) and (5). Why are housing areas in the east rather than the west of Jurong?
2 Why is housing close to light rather than heavy industry?
3 Study photograph (9).
  (a) What type of housing is at A?
  (b) Say why this type of housing is built.
  (c) Suggest the use of the public building at B.
  (d) What types of recreation are shown at C, D and E?

Parks and open spaces

1 The two largest areas of open space in the east and west of the estate are for a golf club and leisure gardens. Which area has which use? Say why.
2 How does the plan allow large numbers of people to have a view over the open space in the east of the estate?
3 Photograph (10) shows the Chinese Garden. What makes this an interesting place to visit?

Town Hall and Centre

1 Study map (5). The Town Hall and Centre were built on the highest land in the east of the estate. Suggest reasons for this decision.
2 Study photograph (11).
  (a) Why is this a suitable site for a town hall but not a factory?
  (b) Suggest the use for the tower on top of the building.

Education

Suggest advantages for each of these:
1 A technical institute on the estate.
2 A university and science park near to the estate.
3 A child day-care centre.

9 Housing and recreation

10 Chinese Garden

Making decisions

Imagine you are a member of the planning board for Jurong industrial estate. Say what decisions you would make on the following matters and give your reasons.

1 In 1989 the newly reclaimed area of land shown on map (5) is ready for use. Should it be used for industry, oil-refining sites, housing, recreation, a nature reserve, or a mix of some of these things?
2 Two sites, marked A and B on map (5), are available for a waste-incineration plant. Which would you choose?
3 There is a plan for a twenty-four-storey block which would include flats, shops, post office and clinic. Would you favour the plan?

11 Jurong Town Hall

SCIENCE PARK

Buildings in pleasant surroundings next to a university, or other place of higher education, where people work in industrial research and development. Industrialists and the university work together, sharing facilities and developing ideas, in electronics for example, which will give rise to new industries or update existing ones on the nearby industrial estates.

Index